BY ANDREW RANNELLS

Uncle of the Year

Too Much Is Not Enough

BY ANDREW RANNELLS

Uncle of the Year

Too Much Is Not Enough

fashion color, like "Sage" or "Coriander," wearing knockoff Adidas soccer shorts and a Creighton Prep Post Prom T-shirt with the sleeves cut off. (The theme was "Arctic Blast." Whatever that means. Don't let straight boys pick prom themes. Leave it to the gays and the girls.)

The phone rang. It was Randi. She was living in San Antonio, Texas, working at Six Flags as a performer. I hadn't seen her in months and was thrilled to get the call. She started in right away with terrifying enthusiasm: "I'm going to be on *Ricki Lake!* They are reuniting me with my ex, Tony!"

"Reuniting" seemed an odd choice of words. As far as I knew, Tony lived a mile away from Randi and one day he had just stopped calling her back. As for "ex," I didn't think that they had been dating that long. But whatever.

"Wow," I said, only partially listening. "When are you going?"

"The day after tomorrow!" she said. "Do you want to come? I have one free companion ticket. It's only forty-eight hours but they are paying for everything. Please say yes!"

Now I was really listening.

I was eighteen, newly finished with high school, and preparing to move to New York for college at the end of the summer. I was not starting my summer job at the Gap for another two weeks, and I had just realized how hideous this bathroom paint color truly was.

"Hell yes, I'll come!"

And that was that. I told my parents that night what I was planning. I did not ask permission, I did not leave any room for negotiation, I just told them I would be gone for forty-eight hours in New York City, alone with a girl who regularly drove the wrong way down one-way streets. Much to my relief (and as I write this, my horror), they didn't say a word except "What time is your flight?" I was off!

I arrived at JFK and there was a man waiting for me with a sign that read, "Andy Rannells." Just like the movies! I had been to New York twice, but this time felt different. It was springtime, it was sunny, and I had a goddamn chauffeur! We pulled up to the nicest hotel I had ever seen. The lobby was decorated with oversized furniture and every wall seemed to be an accent wall in jewel tones. There was a bar in the lobby filled with chic-looking businesspeople, whom I now realize were also visitors to the city, all drinking colorful martinis that were strangely also in jewel tones. It all seemed very glamorous. At the front desk I was told that "Ms. Newton" was already in the room. *Ms. Newton! Fancy!*

When I got to the room, which was small but lovely, Randi was staring tensely out the window. "Hi," she said sort of tentatively. I knew something was up, but I was temporarily distracted by her new look. She had darkened her hair but gotten *extremely* blond, chunky highlights. The effect was very Yasmine Bleeth from *Baywatch*. It suited her. We hugged and chatted about our flights and the hotel and New York, and I started planning activities ("Do you think we'll have time to see *Miss Saigon*?!"). Finally, she looked at me very seriously.

"Andy," she said, "we have to talk."

Goddamn it. Of course this was too good to be true! Was she going to ask me for money? I couldn't afford any of this. Or was it something else? Was Tony here? Was I going to have to get my own room or something?

"Tony refused to come," she said sadly.

"I'm so sorry, Randi." Randi was a flighty gal but very sensitive. Even though her relationship had probably been short-lived, I knew that she felt everything deeply. "Doesn't this sort of put a damper on your reunion though?"

I recognized the look that came over her face. It was a look that I had grown accustomed to over the years. It was a look that said, *I have plotted and planned and may have done something irrational.* Like when she decided to stalk a waiter and made me sit outside his house for hours one night to see if he had a girlfriend. Like the time she wanted me to help her make a "canopy bed" in her room by stapling her curtains to the ceiling. Oh, yes, I knew this look well.

"What did you do?" I asked, terrified of the answer.

"Well . . . ," she started, "I told the producers that I have always had a secret crush on you and I'm going to tell you on the show tomorrow. Please don't be mad. They were going to cancel our trip otherwise!"

I was livid. How could she do this to me? I was supposed to be her companion, to sit in the audience and smile supportively, not be onstage and receive her misplaced and false affections. All the tickets to *Miss Saigon* in the world weren't worth this. How the fuck were we going to get out of this? I went into crisis mode. There had to be a way out. We could fake a death in the family; we could say we got mugged.

"We have to do the show, otherwise they will cancel our tickets and we will have to pay to get home," she said. "I can't afford that. Can you?"

She had a point.

Now, a reasonable eighteen-year-old might have just called his parents and begged for help. Or he might have sucked it up, taken some of his savings, and bought a plane ticket himself. But I was not reasonable. I was trying to be independent, and I was determined to take care of myself. Even if that meant lying to Tracy Turnblad on her talk show.

I started thinking quickly about how to handle this. *We are actors, right? We will just come up with a scene to play—something simple—and just get in, get out, and continue with our trip.* We decided that Randi would confess her love for me, I would act surprised, and I would tell her I loved her as a friend. Then she would act sad, but we would agree that friendship was for the best. I just assumed my natural acting ability would carry us through this nightmare. I mean, I had won an Omaha Theater Arts Guild award for Outstanding Youth Actor in *110 in the Shade*, for Christ's sake. I was the midwestern Mark-Paul Gosselaar as far as I was concerned.

The next morning, a production assistant from the show met us in the hotel lobby. She was pleasant and friendly, but I was too terrified to make any small talk on the ride to the studio. Randi was extremely quiet, too.

It's a miracle I remember anything at all, because I was managing a panic attack throughout the entire taping. I do remember being told that Randi would be in the last segment and thinking that Ricki Lake was as charming and bubbly in person as she was on-screen. She was pretty and seemed sweet and was chatting with the crowd like everyone was her friend. I vaguely recall sitting alone in the audience while guest after guest either reconnected with someone from their romantic past or confessed a crush on someone in their life. I remember none of the details of their stories, what they looked like, nothing.

The show was taped, but it moved in real time. The commercial breaks were the length of real commercial breaks. Everything was moving very quickly. Then, Randi was onstage. Everything sort of slowed down, like in a nightmare where you are being attacked and you can't fight back. Like you are moving underwater while everyone else is moving at normal speed.

I knew that I was about to be on camera, so I tried to act extra natural. I had been in several local television commercials at this point, so I believed I knew what "played." Randi started her story about being single and having trouble finding love. Ricki compared her to Yasmine Bleeth (thanks to Randi's colorist in Texas). And then Ricki asked her if she had brought anyone with her that day. She said yes, her best friend, Andy. Ricki was conveniently standing right next to me and shoved the microphone in my face and asked, "Why do you think your friend is single? She's such a catch." I responded with, in my mind, some bland, supportive comment, and smiled calmly. Then Ricki said, "Randi, do you have something you want to tell Andy?" At this point the crowd went wild. They were like zoo animals at feeding time. They all knew something was about to happen. Something that could potentially end badly, and they were out for blood. "Get on up there onstage, Andy!" Ricki screamed.

The audience started cheering and I, naturally but with an air of slight concern, took my seat on the stage next to Randi. Someone attached a microphone to my lime-green tie from Structure and Randi pulled a letter out from underneath her chair. She then proceeded to read the letter, which explained that she had always loved me but didn't know how to tell me. I found her performance to be a little over-the-top, honestly. I was trying my best to psychically tell her, *Pull back, girl!* But it wasn't working. I also noticed the cameras at this point. There must have been four or five, and they all had red lights on top of them. I gathered that when the light was on, that was the camera that was film-ing. I subtly started to adjust to the movement of the cam-era. I wanted them to catch all this incredible acting I was doing.

When Randi finished, the crowd went wild again. Ricki quieted them down and then said, "Andy, what do you think?" I proceeded to give a *very* natural response, explain-ing that I also loved Randi, but as a friend. The audience booed, Randi looked sad, and then we held hands in a sup-portive show of friendship.

Ricki asked Randi, "No hard feelings?"

Randi shook her head and said she was sad but she un-derstood. Success! We did it! We'd played our scene and now we could get the fuck out of there and get our *Miss Saigon* tickets! But the segment did not end there. Oh no. As you may recall, Ricki often opened the floor up to ques-tions. And this audience, my friends, had questions. Mainly, one young woman who stood up and said, "I have a ques-tion for Andy. I don't mean any disrespect, but are you gay?"

Let's unpack this young woman's phrasing, shall we?

Part one: "I don't mean any disrespect." That means that there is *definitely* something disrespectful about what is about to be said. Like when people use the word "actually" too much. "She's *actually* really pretty." Which essentially means, "I thought she was a fucking beast, but it turns out, not so much." I was already on the defensive.

Part two: "Are you gay?" This clearly means that my performance as "Straight Guy in the Audience of *The Ricki Lake Show*" did not go as planned. I was butching it up, kids! I was hitting you with all the Matt Dillon realness I could muster. But according to this audience member, my hard work was lost in translation. And based on the audience's response, she was not the only person who thought this was a possibility. *Oh no,* I realized. *Everyone knows I am gay.*

I took a moment and tried to decide how to proceed. It crossed my mind that I could use this as a spectacular way to come out, since I had not officially told my family yet. (Although my obsession with Maxwell Caulfield from the age of five had probably tipped them off. . . .) This was 1997, and coming out was still tricky. Families weren't always supportive, and mine deserved to hear it from me in person and not on a television show that featured topics such as "Players Get Played" and "Extreme Breast Makeovers." Had it been Oprah, I would have been waving a rainbow flag while singing "Get Happy" for all to see, but this didn't seem right. So instead, I smiled and said, "No, I just dress well." The crowd went nuts again. Ricki thanked us for coming and introduced a commercial break.

And then silence. For the first time during that taping,

there was total silence. Ricki left, some of the cameramen left, the producers who were in the audience left. Nothing was happening. I knew something was very, very wrong. Randi and I didn't speak to each other; we didn't even look at each other. The audience was just staring at us. Then, everyone who had left returned. Our microphones were taken off and we were whisked backstage to a greenroom with the other guests. They all smiled at us awkwardly. No one spoke to us.

Ricki ended the show and then someone came backstage to take everyone to their cars and back to the hotel. Except for us. Randi and I were left sitting in the greenroom alone. I knew this was bad. This was very bad. A group of about ten people walked into the room. I had never met a producer or an executive from a network, but I knew I was looking at them right now. An older woman spoke. "We know you two are lying and we do not tolerate that on *The Ricki Lake Show*. We have integrity here." I wanted to argue her point, as I had recently watched an episode called "I'm a Queen in Drag and I'm Fat and All That," but I held my tongue. "We can't air this show because you were clearly lying. We are prepared to sue you for the cost of production, which is over a million dollars. Do you understand that?"

Now, you might think that this is where Randi and I break. That we collapse in a puddle and plead for forgiveness and understanding, citing naïveté or poor parenting or the societal pressures that led us to this point. But no, that's not what happened. Instead, Randi burst into tears. "I was just humiliated on national television! Do you think I would willingly put myself in that position? That's absurd!" I followed her lead.

"I am from Omaha, Nebraska, and I was just outed on TV! My parents are going to disown me! I don't know if I can even go back there! When this airs, they will never speak to me again!" Now we were both crying and shouting over each other about how this was a huge mistake and we never should have come here, how I was lied to and tricked. Then Randi really brought the hammer down. "I wanted to be reunited with my ex and instead you bullied me into confessing a crush that I don't even have. This was all your idea!"

That's when the air in the room shifted. They *had* changed gears awfully quickly with Randi, and had allowed her to completely change her story at the last minute so they wouldn't lose a guest. She had them by the balls. Everyone started to back away from us. "Okay," the producer said, "we are sorry you both feel hurt by this experience. Thank you for coming though. Enjoy the rest of your time in New York." They all left the room.

A production assistant came in and took us to our car. We rode in total silence, afraid to speak. What had we done? What had we gotten away with? We got to the hotel, but we didn't go to the room. Randi mouthed to me,

"What if the room is bugged?" A rather ludicrous sugges-
tion, but we weren't taking any chances. We walked to a
coffee shop instead. Once we saw the driver was gone, we
burst into laughter. We cried, hugged, vacillated between
relief and terror. We congratulated each other on disarm-
ing the situation and agreed that we couldn't ever speak of
this. We wouldn't tell anyone we had done it and we would
just pretend that it had never happened. How many people watched *Ricki Lake* anyway? It couldn't be that many.
Most important, we were going to walk to TKTS to get
Miss Saigon tickets for that night. Everything was going to
be fine.

Months later, the show aired. I was just about to leave
for New York and Randi was still in San Antonio. She had
kept track of the airdate through *TV Guide* and called me
when she saw our episode was going to air. I didn't want to
watch it. I had mostly put it behind me and really willed
myself into believing that nothing bad had happened. I sat
down alone to watch what I was certain was a stellar and
naturalistic performance.

It turns out . . . what's the best way to say this? You
know when there's a talk show *within* a movie, or a movie
within a TV show, and it always just seems off? That's what
this was. Randi and I were performing so hard it was as if
we were in a skit on *The Carol Burnett Show*. She was doing
some weird affectation and tossing her hair around, I was
speaking directly into the camera every time it adjusted,

and I seemed so stilted and fake, and, not for nothing, gayer than Paul Lynde at Palm Springs Pride! I don't know who I thought I was fooling, because it seemed like it was just myself. The only comfort I could find was in the fact that it was over. I didn't know anyone who watched the show, so I didn't feel too in danger of anyone's seeing it. I could just put this whole episode behind me now and focus on my new life in New York City.

Once I got to New York, I quickly found out who watches *The Ricki Lake Show:* people who live in New York! I was recognized constantly on the subway. "You were on *Ricki!*" Or "You're the gay guy from *Ricki!*" Or just, "You're that gay guy!" It was a type of fame that I definitely did not want and was not thrilled by. Luckily, it only lasted a couple of weeks, though I did have to throw away that lime-green Structure tie, which was probably for the best.

Eight months later, *The Ricki Lake Show* reached out to Randi to see if we wanted to come back on the show. Apparently, we had received a lot of fan mail and they wanted us to play the *Dating Game* on the show with viewers who wanted to meet us. Two guys for Randi and, you guessed it, two guys for me. It was a definite pass for me, but Randi agreed and went back on the show. She later told me the producers were all very friendly and so thrilled to see her. Apparently their professional integrity was outweighed by the positive viewer response.

When I look back now at my first time on national television, I'm not proud of it. First of all, I gave a lousy performance, and second, I was lousy at playing myself! Or the version of myself I thought I had to be in that moment. I did want to be on television again one day, but I definitely didn't want to do it like that. It made me vow to myself that the next time I was going to be on TV, it would be because I was acting in something. And if I was ever on television as Andrew Rannells, I was going to be the *real* Andrew Rannells. The Andrew I was proud of.

I did get to see *Miss Saigon* with Matt Bogart and Deedee Lynn Magno (from *The All New Mickey Mouse Club*) and I adored every second of it. Was it worth the public humiliation on *Ricki Lake*? Probably not. But it was damn close.

THE CHRISTIAN,
HIS WIFE, AND ME

———

'VE CHANGED SOME NAMES AND DETAILS IN THIS ESSAY because it's the type of essay that requires some name changing. In fact, I wish I could change my own name, but I am the one writing it, so I'm kind of stuck.

Devin and I had been working out of town together for months. Both of us were seemingly far away from home and working in a lovely but still slightly busted regional theater, "paying our dues," as they say in showbiz.

I liked Devin. He was easy to work with and great in the show, a dusty musical that was desperately trying to be reinvented by an overly ambitious creative team. I admired how steady he was, onstage and off, but I didn't really socialize much with him because A) he didn't really socialize with anyone, and B) he was married and *very* Christian. He was extremely vocal about his religious commitment and always prayed before we started each show. He would sometimes see me and the rest of the cast stumbling home from a night out, and while he would smile and ask how our time was, I got the strong sense that he would later be praying for our souls. His wife, Anne, was sweet. Like diabetically sweet. She had visited twice and was lovely both times, but she seemed to be dancing as fast as she could every second of the day. She dressed in 1950s-style dresses, with a makeup plot to match. She was always hot-rollered and perfumed and smiling so hard I thought her teeth would crack. They were a cute couple. They seemed happy together, or at least content.

I'll be honest, I didn't give Devin and Anne much thought at first. I was very involved with my own offstage activities and had recently decided to try dating again after a difficult breakup. I had met two very different men who both asked me out the same week. I decided that I should give each of them a try. Bachelor #1 was a man in his mid-forties who owned a few gay bars around town. He was charming and handsome and had a swagger that suggested that he either had the biggest dick in the state or was extremely wealthy. Or both. (I quickly found out the answer was both.) Bachelor #2 was a twenty-three-year-old barista at Starbucks who was studying classical literature. He was a little shy, was very sweet, and had an aura about him that made you want to be close to him, to protect him. Both of these men had potential, but the show took up the majority of my time, so neither relationship generated much momentum. But that was okay with me since I was just dipping my toe back in the dating scene. I was from out of town. What kind of shelf life could either of these relationships have anyway?

Then, one evening after the show, Devin asked me where everyone was going out that night. Surprisingly, he wanted to join us. "I want to blow off some steam," he said. I was thrilled he wanted to come. He always seemed a little tightly wound, and his wife had just been visiting, so no one had seen much of him offstage recently.

So that night, we all went out to a dive bar near the theater. The staff there had grown accustomed to our post-show visits and even greeted us by name when we arrived. As was the tradition, everyone began drinking at breakneck speed, but the real surprise was, Devin started drinking heavily, too, suggesting shots to get the evening started. I am not really a shot guy, but there was something so celebratory about Devin that everyone just went with it, myself included. It felt like it was his birthday or his last night before going to jail. Needless to say, everyone was drunk in record time. I should note that there was no food at this bar. In my experience, a lot of actors prefer that method of drunkenness: Save the calories for the booze.

A couple of hours in, I went into the bathroom. I always liked to try to gauge, based on my appearance in the mirror, whether I *looked* drunk. "Is this what I look like drunk?" I would ask myself. Then I'd adjust my hair, pinch my cheeks, and tell myself, "You're good! You look totally sober!" I almost believed it. While I was going through this ritual, Devin entered the bathroom. While he was standing at the urinal he asked me, "Are you having fun?"

"I'm having a great time, Devin. What about you?"

"I am having the best time, Andrew. I don't know why I don't go out with you guys more often. Anne doesn't like it when I go out. She doesn't really like it when I drink."

"That's too bad," I replied absentmindedly while playing with my hair in the mirror. *Am I losing my hair?* I wondered. *According to my genes, I should just go gray. I don't know. Maybe I should start Propecia.*

"I hope I'm not making a fool out of myself tonight," Devin said, now washing his hands next to me. "I'm just trying to have fun."

"You're fine!" I said. "You should have fun. You are working very hard, Devin. You need some time to unwind."

"You're right," he said.

And then, ladies and gentlemen of the jury, with the speed and precision of a ninja, Devin's tongue was in my mouth. He pressed me up against the wall of the bathroom and was grinding against me. He was like an octopus; his hands were suddenly everywhere. He was a very good kisser, very passionate and very enthusiastic. The bathroom door swung open. With the same speed and exactness, Devin was back at the sink washing his hands. I was still against the wall, too shocked to move. Rob, one of our cast-mates, strutted in, oblivious to the energy hanging in the room. He shouted as he peed, "We're all going back to the hotel to get one more drink. Let's go!"

"Sounds good to me," Devin said. And then he smiled at me in the mirror.

I was floored. What had just happened? Had something happened, or had I just hallucinated that? What exactly was in the Redheaded Slut shots I had done at the bar?

We all walked to the hotel in a group, Devin somewhere behind me, laughing and talking with other folks. I was walking with two women, trying my best to help them navigate the sidewalk in their heels. We got to the hotel bar and Devin ordered everyone a round. He handed me my drink.

"Can we do more of that later?" he kind of whispered to me.

I looked at his face. He was smiling and he sort of had two heads as my eyes struggled to focus on his features. He looked different, more relaxed. He didn't look like the Devin I thought I knew.

"Sure," I said. Although I'm pretty positive it sounded more like "Shhhhhuuure." I was drunk. He was drunk. And we were just getting drunker.

I lost time that evening. Which is a polite way to say I blacked out. Not a full blackout, more like rolling black-outs. There are little snippets of time that are very clear in my head, and then stretches of time that are a complete blank. For instance, I have a clear recollection of Rob shouting at us as we were leaving the hotel bar, "Where are you guys going?!" Then I have no memory of the elevator ride or opening the door to my room.

I remember Devin holding my face and saying, "I've wanted to kiss you since the day I met you."

I don't know how we both came to be fully naked and having sex in front of the bathroom mirror. But I remember the mirror part.

I remember rolling around in my bed doing all the sex things we could possibly do. But I don't remember falling asleep.

I *do* remember waking up though. Slowly, calmly, I opened my eyes, and then . . . WHAM! Most of the events of the night before smacked me in the face. I lay very still in the bed, afraid to move. Uncertain of what lay next to me, I quietly adjusted my body so I could see the other side of the bed. The room was pitch-black. I don't remember shutting the curtains, but I was pleased that I had. The bed was empty. I got up to look in the bathroom. The bathroom was empty. "Devin?" I said to no one. "Devin?" I asked again, just in case he was hiding, although there was no place to hide.

I opened the curtains and temporarily blinded myself. As my eyes started to adjust, I was able to piece together the crime scene. Apparently, we had opened a bottle of wine from the minibar. Great decision. There were clothes and shoes strewn about. Sheets and blankets on the floor. And then I noticed something truly odd. Those weren't my shoes. That wasn't my shirt. Those weren't my jeans. They were Devin's. Devin's jacket. Devin's underwear. Devin's wallet. Devin's cell phone. But where the fuck was Devin? My mind started racing. Still slightly drunk, I tried to think of what to do. I called his hotel room phone. There was no answer. I called again. No answer. I threw on a robe and carefully opened the door to my room, my thought being, *Maybe he got confused in the night and mistook the front door for the bathroom and is now locked out, naked and lying in the hallway.*

He was not naked in the hall, much to my relief. But maybe he *had been* naked in the hall and someone had called security. Maybe he was in hotel jail, or real jail for that matter. Maybe I had slept through all the hallway ker-fuffle. How would I find this out? I couldn't call him; his phone was right in front of me. I would have to call the front desk.

"Hello. This is Andrew Rannells in eleven oh six. I have a strange question. Were there any incidents that occurred overnight?"

"Like what kind of incidents?" the receptionist droned.

"Oh, I don't know, like . . . anything that involved the police or security or anyone being naked in the lobby?" I felt like I was Guy Pearce in *Memento*.

"Ummm . . . I don't think so," the receptionist said. "I just started, let me ask Tom." I didn't know who Tom was, but I was hopeful he could be helpful. "Tom!" she yelled. "Was anybody naked down here last night?" There was a brief pause. "Tom says no."

"Thank you!" I said. "And thank Tom!"

I hung up, humiliated but relieved. I sat on the bed racking my brain about what to do next. Devin was somewhere out there, naked and afraid. What would a married Christian guy do the morning after having sex with a man for the first time? Well, it was *definitely* not his first time. No one is that skilled or adventurous their first time.

Then I noticed something. Where were my clothes? Where were my shoes? My coat? I looked in the closet. I was often very tidy while drunk, but no such luck this time. My wallet and phone were on the nightstand, but the clothing I had been wearing was gone. Even my underwear and socks. Did he wear my clothes to go back to his room? What would the point of that be?

I decided to go to his room. I got dressed, gathered up Devin's clothes, and made my way through the hotel. It was only seven-thirty in the morning so I doubted I would see anyone from our show. I got to Devin's room and prayed he was there. I knocked. I knocked louder. I knocked again, and then I heard movement from within the room. The door slowly opened and there was Devin, looking sheepish and kind of scared and wearing only my underwear.

"Come in," he said.

"Are you okay?" I asked, already knowing the answer.

Then, much to my surprise, he kissed me again. Like, really kissed me. *I should have brushed my teeth,* I thought. He fell into me and I held him tightly. He squeezed me back. He started crying. Hard. "I'm so sorry, Andrew. I'm so sorry."

I held him tighter. I didn't know Devin very well. And yet I did in other ways. I now knew something very personal about him and I felt protective of that. I wanted him to be okay.

"Who knows? Who saw us?" he asked through his tears.

"I don't really remember," I said. "Maybe Rob?"

"Shit, shit, shit," he kept saying.

I held his face in my hands. "No one needs to know about this, Devin. No one. It was just us in that room. Definitely no one knows what happened between us. Let's just say you walked me to my room. I was drunk. You were drunk. You were helping me out. That's it."

He started crying harder. He kissed me again. I kissed him back. We held each other for what felt like a long time. Then he said, "So we can just not tell anyone?"

"Yes! No one needs to know."

"What about Anne?" he cried.

I was torn. Even though I was the embodiment of this man's stress and confusion, I also wanted to be his friend and help him figure out what the next best steps might be.

I thought about what we'd done, whom it affected. I thought about his life with Anne, her feelings, their life. And then I thought, *It's not worth blowing all that up because of one drunken night.* Neither of us was going to get pregnant, I had no diseases to share, no one else knew what had gone on between us. Devin definitely needed to do some soul-searching as to why he wanted to do what he did, but a night of sloppily working his way through the gay Kama Sutra with me wasn't a good way to start that conversation with his wife. I knew I wouldn't tell anyone, so I decided, *Let's bury this for the moment. Let's bury it deep and dig it up another day when our heads are clearer.*

"Don't tell her," I said calmly.

He looked me right in the eyes. He looked sad. He looked scared. And then he looked relieved.

"Okay. I won't."

He kissed me again. We held each other some more and then I started to leave. I stopped.

"Can I get my clothes back?"

"Oh. Sure." He kind of laughed. He piled my clothes together and put them in my arms. I thought about asking for my underwear, but then I thought better of it.

I left in a total haze. What had just happened? And how did I feel about it? Was I a horrible person? Maybe. Was this my fault? Possibly. Should I have behaved differently? Yes. But here we were.

That night at the show, I didn't speak to Devin before

we started. In fact, I didn't even see him. We spotted each other for the first time since that morning onstage, wearing other people's clothes, using other people's names, and inhabiting other people's personalities. *Everything is normal,* I thought. *It's like nothing happened.*

I went to my dressing room at intermission. I had successfully pushed the day's events out of my mind while at work. That was for the best. I picked up my phone. Twenty-two new text messages. My blood went cold. I knew exactly what this was. Who this was.

All the texts were from the same unknown number. The first text read, "Andrew, this is Anne. Devin's wife. You are a godless fucking whore." It went on from there. Text after text, all with the same fervor. The same rage and different creative ways to say, "whore." Then around text eighteen, the tone shifted. "I've been praying for you and I am ready to forgive you." The first act was ninety minutes, so she had really been through quite a journey in a relatively short period of time. "Devin and I will get through this with the help of Jesus. And Jesus will help you and forgive you if you open your heart."

I was floored. I read them all again, trying to piece together her mental state. I couldn't understand how she had made the jump to forgiveness so quickly. Was it the power of Jesus, or had a Xanax kicked in mid–text rage? I went over to Devin's dressing room. Before I could say anything, he said, "I had to tell her. I'm sorry."

"What am I supposed to say to her? How do I respond to this?" I showed him my phone. His face got red.

"I'm sorry," he said. "I'm not supposed to talk to you offstage anymore. And I definitely can't be alone with you. You have to leave."

"Are you serious?" I asked. But I knew he was.

"Yes. Please leave. I'm sorry."

I walked back to my dressing room a little pissed, a little ashamed, a little numb. I knew I needed to respond to Anne, but I didn't know what to say. I finally typed, "Anne, I don't know what to say. I acted irresponsibly and selfishly. I am grateful for your forgiveness." And that was it.

"Places for the top act two! Places!" sounded over the theater's PA system. It was time to go back to work and forget this disaster for the duration of the performance. When I returned to my dressing room after the show, there was another message from Anne. Just one. It read, "I'm on my way to see Devin. I would like to speak to you in person."

It was at this moment that I truly realized what I had done, what my actions actually meant. This was not just some drunken fling that I could brush off. This was two people's lives; this involved someone else's personal struggle; this was someone else's husband. I felt like an asshole. I called Zuzanna. She didn't know any of the other players, so I knew she could be impartial and wouldn't tell anyone. I told her the whole story. "Holy shit" was all she could say.

Then I asked her how to handle it and what to say to this woman. She thought about it. "Apologize and listen to what she has to say and be respectful of how they want to move forward." She was right. That was precisely what I needed to do.

Anne arrived the next day. Devin texted and asked if I could meet them in the lobby of the hotel. I was a little shocked but also relieved that we were going to have this chat in such a public place. I made my way to the lobby, and there were Devin and Anne. Anne was, as usual, dressed like she was in a production of *How to Succeed in Business Without Really Trying*. Her hair was curled and pulled to the side. Her makeup was thick and very exact. She was smiling the kind of huge smile people use when greeting a favorite nephew or a beloved grandparent. Devin was completely ashen. He was wearing a rumpled T-shirt and baggy jeans. He seemed unshowered and was staring at the floor. His eyes were red and puffy. He never looked up at me. Not once.

Anne stood up to greet me and hugged me tightly. Very tightly. Like she might be trying to crack my ribs. She whispered in my ear, "I forgive you." I was relieved but also suspicious. How could she have come around so quickly? Jesus was really working overtime, I guess. Then she held me at arm's length and said, "This is an issue that Devin and I are going to work through with our pastor and God. We would both really appreciate you not mentioning this incident to anyone. Also, I hope you understand that you can't have any contact with Devin offstage. Absolutely none. I'm sure you can respect that."

"Of course," I said. "I want to say—" She cut me off.

"No need to say anything. We are all moving forward, so I suggest you do the same. Have a great show tonight!"

That was that. I smiled; I looked at Devin, who was still staring at the ground; and then I walked back to my room. We were moving forward.

Devin called in sick to the show that night, so his understudy went on. I wasn't surprised, and it was for the best. When I got to my dressing room there was a manila envelope at my makeup table. "Andrew Rannells" was written across it in black Sharpie. I opened it up, not sure of what it could be. It was my underwear from that night with Devin. Washed and neatly folded. She must have done it. She must have washed it, put it in that envelope, and delivered it to the theater that day. Such a complicated and personal chore. If I were her, I just would have thrown them away. If I were him, I *definitely* would have. I certainly wouldn't have mentioned that I still had them. It was all very strange. And sad.

The rest of the run of the show, I did as I was told. I stayed away from Devin and only interacted with him onstage. He made himself scarce offstage, never socializing with the rest of the cast again. It made me sad for him. It made me sad for Anne, too. He clearly wasn't where he

wanted to be, and Anne deserved better. They both deserved to be living their lives authentically and honestly
with partners who fully accepted them. But what did I
know? I was no authority on relationships. It made me
wonder if this type of compromise, this level of forgiveness,
was what it took to have a successful, albeit fraught, long-
term relationship. The level of guilt I felt about the whole
ordeal—thank you, Catholicism—was overwhelming, so I
could only imagine what Devin was feeling. At the same
time, I had been cheated on in the past, so I could also understand Anne's devastation. And yet they were moving
forward together. Was that bravery? Was that commitment? Was that foolishness? I didn't know. I still don't.

The closing night of the show I decided that I needed to
talk to Devin alone. I was his friend, and while I had complicated his marriage, I also cared about him and wanted to
see how he was doing. I didn't know what to say, but I felt
like I should at least try to close this chapter, if that was
possible. Fifteen minutes before the show started, I went to
his dressing room and knocked on the door. He answered
and looked a little surprised and then said, "Come in." He
shut the door quickly behind me. We both stared at each
other for a moment and then he hugged me tightly. I held
him back. Then something unexpected happened: I started
to cry. And then he started to cry. I felt terrible about all of
it, and I felt terrible for him. I can't say why he was crying,
but I imagine it was a version of my reason.

"Thank you," he said. For what? I'm not sure. I didn't ask for more, nor did I offer anything else. I just left the room.

In the months that followed I would occasionally see Devin and Anne back at home. As fate would have it, we lived blocks away from one another. We would never stop and chat; it was always just a quick hello and a tense smile. I think that's all anyone could manage. About a year later, I saw them again, and this time Anne was pregnant. They were moving forward together.

Good for them, I guess. Good for them.

THINGS YOU LEARN AT AN UNDERWEAR PARTY

LIKE TO THINK OF MYSELF AS A FREE SPIRIT. SOMEONE who goes with the flow of life. A real "Yes, and" kind of guy. But the truth is I am not. I like rules, I like instruction, I love a list of things to do and a well-thought-out plan.

This tension deep inside me is best explained by the movie *Mystic Pizza*. As a kid, I loved the film and desperately wanted to be Julia Roberts's character, Daisy—fun and spontaneous, with wild hair and a propensity for outrageous (and sometimes irrational) behavior and questionable fashion choices. I turned out to be more like Annabeth Gish's character, Kat. A nerdy but sexually ambitious astronomy student who always shows up on time and is available to cover your shift at the pizza joint at the last minute. I mention this because A) I don't think *Mystic Pizza* is referenced enough in the zeitgeist and B) I want to give you a little context as to what my natural social instincts are.

For most of my life, I have gravitated toward the comfortable friendship of girls like Daisy and Kat. Maybe it's because they represent the two sides of my personality. Maybe it's because I have three sisters. Or maybe it's just too much *Mystic Pizza*. Either way, there is a safety in hanging out with girls that I learned about at a young age. When I was a little gay boy, girls were way less judgy about my desire to play with Barbies, and I never feared that they might beat me up unexpectedly. They never asked me to play a sport, and they generally admired my wit and knowledge of facts about the cast of *Kids Incorporated*.

As I got older though, I realized that I wanted to have gay friends, too. I thought it might be helpful for my own development as a gay man and would help me feel part of a community in New York. *I should be with my people! But where do I meet them?* I wondered. *How can I find some gay friends?*

For me, the answer was easy: Ask a girl who does a lot of musical theater! They usually have lots of gay friends! Lucky for me, I was already friends with the perfect girl, Jenn. We had met doing summer stock in the Berkshires after my freshman year of college and become close. Jenn's issue was the opposite of mine; she was a gal who almost exclusively hung out with gay men. (She is a brassy belter; that's probably why.)

Through Jenn I met many gay men who strangely also didn't have a ton of other gay friends, and two, Sean and Gavin, quickly became constants in my life. We all started spending a lot of time together, at first with Jenn and then eventually without Jenn. Truth be told, like something out of an '00s romcom, Jenn introduced us all as potential romantic partners. Her thought was, "You're gay! He's gay! You should date!" Alas, gays, like snowflakes, are all unique, and you can't just shove two together and expect them to match, though she certainly tried.

Gavin, Sean, and I started going out together to gay bars, parties, all the things that many gay men in big cities do in their twenties. *We* just hadn't done them yet. And once we started, we *really* got started. We visited all the gay bars in our neighborhood of Hell's Kitchen: Therapy, Barrage, Posh—we hit them all! We ventured into Chelsea and went to Splash, XL, and G Lounge. (If you are gay and lived in New York in the early 2000s, after reading those names I'm sure you can smell the Acqua di Gio.) All those places were great, and we had some fantastic nights at each of them, but before long we'd had our fill of hanging out with hopeful chorus boys in sleeveless Abercrombie T-shirts. We decided we were ready to break out of our comfort zone.

One night, Gavin told us that he'd heard about a bar in the East Village called Opaline. The East Village seemed very edgy for three Hell's Kitchen theater gays, but we were up for the adventure. It turned out to be worth the subway ride, because we had a blast. It was an incredibly fun, specifically gay dance club on Friday nights, and the three of us would dance to the "Milkshake"/"Holiday" mash-up, make out with the occasional boy, and give out a number here and there, but usually split a cab home at the end of the night.

At the time, Gavin and I lived in cramped side-by-side studio apartments on the corner of Forty-fifth Street and Ninth Avenue. My place had a half refrigerator and barely any closet space, and I think it's my favorite place I have ever lived. That's another thing Jenn gave us, that building. I think she was the first to move in, followed by Gavin and then me. Sean was the only one who never moved there, but he spent about every weekend in one of our places anyway. Since most of us lived there, we would end or start most days at the Westway Diner across the street. We called it "the cafeteria," and we would end up there nearly every night, hatching our plans to try out new bars, new experiences. (Zuzanna stayed with me there for several weeks while she was on break from grad school, and she said it was like living on a cruise ship: tiny rooms, same people, same dining room every day, and a lot of booze.)

I am pretty certain it was Sean who found the Slide, which was also in the East Village. The Slide was in a basement that you could only access by one decrepit staircase that was lit by red lightbulbs. It immediately smelled like sour bar fruit and BO mixed with a hint of Brut deodorant. As we waited for the doorman to check our IDs, I could see that the Slide attracted a slightly different clientele from Opaline. There were more tattoos, and everyone seemed like they were some kind of "found object" art installer who had never been above Fourteenth Street. It was an intimidating crowd. They seemed slightly dangerous, not in a "they might stab us" kind of way, more like a "they might make fun of us if we don't know what every color of the hanky code means" kind of way. Keep in mind that I still looked like a Precious Moments confirmation cake topper. I wasn't exactly blending in. The doorman gave us a quick up-and-down and was probably thinking I had gotten lost on my way to a show choir conference. (Quick side note: The doorman at this bar was none other than now-famous actor and all-around dreamboat Murray Bartlett. Years later I would go on to work with and befriend Murray, but at this point he was just an aspirational hunk whom I desperately wanted to notice me. Spoiler: He did not notice me.)

Once we were past the doorman, a guy near the front door handed us small trash bags.

"What are these for?" I asked.

"They are for your clothes," he said. "It's Underwear Night."

Panic streaked through me. *I can't do that. I was an altar boy!* But before I could protest, and without any conversation, Sean and Gavin just started taking off their clothes. *Are we really going to do this?* The answer was apparently yes. I was immediately sent into a spiral of insecurity, but not wanting to spoil the adventure, I ignored my instincts and off came the clothes. (Except for our shoes and socks. There was still some level of civility.) We put our clothes in the bag, the guy by the door wrote a "bag check" number on our arms, and in we went. There was some concern about where to put my wallet. I settled on my sock. That seemed responsible.

Once inside I was surprised to see it was pretty much business as usual at the Slide, except everyone was in their underwear. It was really weird seeing guys just standing around the bar in their unmentionables, but I loved clocking the kinds of underwear people had on, the colors, the shapes. They promised some insight into what people's personalities might be. Boxer briefs? Probably works in finance and loves Dave Matthews. Briefs? More adventurous and definitely has a share on Fire Island. A jockstrap? We get it, girl. Since we hadn't known what we were walking into that night, I hadn't had the luxury of plotting out what my underwear might be saying about me. Luckily it was 2002, so I was wearing what most guys wore then: black Calvin Klein briefs. Basic, functional, and, I convinced myself, sexually vague in a good way.

We ordered our drinks and stood around trying to act normal. And you know what? Eventually, it did seem normal. You sort of forgot after a few minutes that you didn't have clothes on. It was liberating actually! It felt like a secret society, something slightly shocking to be a part of. We started talking to people, dancing, laughing, really having a good time. All these intimidating people turned out to be fun and silly and more like me than I'd imagined. They were artists and creative types who were all just trying to have fun. I loosened up and let my guard down. I leaned the fuck in! I was in a slightly shady bar, in my underwear, surrounded by strangers, and I was loving it.

For anyone reading this who might have actually been to the Slide around 2002—or a bar like it—you know that there was also a lot of more risqué behavior taking place in the darkest corners. It was shocking but titillating and only added to the spirit of freeness in the air. But for the purpose of this story, we are going to just keep it PG-13 and plow right past those details! The point is, we were having fun and allowing ourselves to stray way out of our comfort zones, especially me.

It was getting late, and by that I mean early, so Sean, Gavin, and I made our way back to the clothes check, where we started to get dressed. "I had a good time!" I told the boys. "I thought it was going to be scary but it wasn't! I would totally come back!" As I was buttoning up my H&M blouse, I realized something . . . my wallet was gone. It must have fallen out of my sock! It had seemed like such a secure location! Or worse, someone had stolen it. All my joy from seconds earlier evaporated and was instantly replaced by midwestern rage/aggressive Catholic guilt. A powerful combo platter of emotion! I spiraled into a judgment-filled internal monologue:

Of course I got my wallet stolen here! I'm surrounded by thieves and whores. Why did I ever think that it would be safe to interact with these people? Why did I even come to the East Village?! This is my punishment for so carelessly leaving the safety of my midtown neighborhood and willingly stripping down to my Calvins in the entryway of a filthy bar where I probably got MRSA, most likely was exposed to hantavirus, and definitely got my wallet stolen. It was probably by that guy who spoke with a French accent but also said he was from Michigan that I impulsively made out with when a remix of "Creep" started playing. This lost wallet is a smackdown from all my dead grandparents who are watching me in heaven saying, "What has happened to Andy? He was such a good boy, and now he's wearing his underwear in public and getting drunk on vodka cranberries purchased for him by a man who looks like Robert Sean Leonard if he worked at a Renaissance fair!" Damn it, I've really done it now. I should have listened to my gut and left the Underwear Party at the Slide as soon as I walked in. It serves me right. This is what I deserve for acting like such a dick.

(FYI, this rant of self-flagellation took place silently and rather quickly. I didn't even tell Sean and Gavin I had lost my wallet. They were talking about some guy with a chain that went from his nipple piercings down to his Prince Albert or some bullshit while I was privately checking myself into rehab and then a monastery.)

I was about to admit to my friends that something horrible had happened, that it was all my fault for being so careless, and that I was vowing to never come to the East Village again or attend another underwear party—and probably should just teach crafts in a senior center for the rest of my life—when someone tapped me on the shoulder. I turned to find an Elijah Wood–looking fella, covered in sweat and glitter and wearing what looked like homemade fairy wings. "I think this is yours," he said with a smile. "I saw it fall out of your sock when you were changing. You should keep it in your underwear." He told me this as he patted his crotch, where there was clearly the shape of a wallet. Before I could thank this Good Samaritan little fairy, he was back on the dance floor twirling away to the Scissor Sisters.

I looked at my wallet. It was indeed mine. I looked to see if my cash and credit cards were still in there. They indeed were. And then I felt a wave of embarrassment mixed with relief wash over me. I hadn't been punished after all! I had learned a lesson about wallet placement when you have no pockets, and everything was okay in the end. My faith in humanity, especially humanity in the East Village, was restored. Maybe *this* was the gift from my dead grandparents! They were telling me, "You can go out and have fun, but keep your shit tight and watch yourself, Andy! This lesson is a freebie on us!"

I finished getting dressed, refreshed and invigorated by our adventure. I took another look at the dance floor and instantly regretted what I'd been thinking a minute before. I saw a beautiful mix of people of all races and sizes, all in their underwear and dancing wildly and freely together. Everyone was in their most basic form (nearly), with nothing to hide physically, and living in that exact moment with unadulterated joy. And when you didn't expect it, they were looking out for one another. It was a beautiful sight and I was also a part of it, a part of that community. I felt the joy and freedom and responsibility that came with being with other people who were like me.

Gavin shouted to me over the music, "You ready to go?"

I smiled back.

"Yeah. But when are we coming back?"

THANK YOU, NEXT!

———

"**T**HEY REALLY LIKED YOU. BUT YOU ARE JUST TOO tall."

That was the feedback that I used to get frequently in theater. I was apparently too much of a giant to play all sorts of parts. I auditioned for a community theater production of *The Skin of Our Teeth*. Too tall. *The Fantasticks* off-Broadway. Too tall. *110 in the Shade* on Broadway. Too tall. (The director, Lonny Price, also told me that I was "too cheesy," so I guess that was part of the problem, too.) Never mind how I sounded when I sang or what kind of perspective I brought to the character through my acting; "too tall" was often the succinct response I would receive. There was really no adjustment I could personally make for that. There wasn't an acting class I could find in *Backstage* called "How to Be Shorter."

Over the course of my career, I've auditioned many times and have received a lot more nos than yeses. I looked too young to understudy Roger in *Rent*. I looked too old to even be seen for *Spring Awakening*. I wasn't "straight-acting" enough to ever be seen for *Mamma Mia*. (Honestly, I didn't know there were any straight people IN *Mamma Mia*.) I was too straight-acting to be cast in *Taboo*. I was never given an audition for *Legally Blonde* or *Catch Me If You Can*, even though I was in *Hairspray* with folks on both creative teams. My voice was too pop for *Les Mis* and *South Pacific*. My voice was too Broadway for *American Idiot*.

Every time I think I am getting ahead, when I think maybe the audition game is over, another one will pop up. Some new hurdle to jump. I don't think that will ever end. You always have to fight for something as an actor; there is always something to be proven. A few auditions have stung more than others, but they've also taught me some valuable lessons.

Let's begin with *Wicked*. That green witch has just kept on calling and stringing me along for years. With every callback I thought, *This time I'm getting it. This time is MY time.* Each time, I was disappointed, but when I look back now, one particular attempt stands out.

When you audition for *Wicked*, you sing and read first for the associate director, Lisa. Usually for me, the process stopped there. But one time, she immediately told me they were bringing me back to meet the director, Joe Mantello.

I was thrilled and nervous about meeting him. He's a legend as a director and an actor.

The day of my callback, I felt ready. There were a couple of other guys in the waiting room, but I wasn't worried. I was just going to go meet Joe Mantello and claim my rightful place in Oz! Lisa came out of the audition room to get me. Clearly, I was her favorite. But something was different about her on this day. She was still friendly but . . . less so. She said, "Just go in there and do exactly what you did last time. Just *exactly* what you did and you'll be fine. Ready?" I nodded. Suddenly, I panicked. *What I did last time? Do I remember what that was? I do, right? It was only five days ago. I have to be able to re-create whatever that magic was.*

Then Lisa did something truly odd, absolutely stunning, and incredibly jarring. She looked me square in the eyes, licked her thumb, and then ran it down my cheek, leaving a wet streak of saliva on my face. Then she looked at her thumb, shrugged, and said, "So you aren't wearing makeup? Your skin is great." I didn't know what had just happened. Was I supposed to wear makeup? Would it be rude to immediately wipe her saliva off my face? And most important . . . WHO DOES THAT TO ANOTHER PERSON WHO IS NOT THEIR OWN TODDLER?!

I don't remember the audition itself. I know I did it, but it was not magical. I did not feel good, and I left knowing that I did not book it. A day later that feeling was confirmed when my agent called to share the bad news. He told me, "Casting said that Joe Mantello said you were good, but you seemed self-conscious." I *was* self-conscious! I had a stranger's spit on my face! I felt betrayed. That was supposed to be my job!

After that disaster, I made a pact with myself that I didn't want to audition to be a replacement anymore. I wanted to originate roles, or at least revive them in a new production. I wanted to do something that I could put my stamp on. I told my agent, and much to my relief, he agreed with me.

My next notable audition was for Conrad Birdie in the revival of *Bye Bye Birdie* for the Roundabout. I made it through many callbacks until it was just me and a very talented actor named Ben Walker. (This was before *Bloody Bloody Andrew Jackson*.) We read, we sang, and then we danced together. Ben was great and very friendly, and I remember riding down in the elevator with him and thinking, *Well, it's one of us, and he seems like a really nice guy if he gets it.* A couple of days went by and then my agent called. Conrad Birdie would not be going to me or Ben Walker. Instead they'd hired a young man who was on a Nickelodeon show. Which show? Who knows? But he was on a TV show.

At that point, I decided I should be on a show. The problem was that I didn't have any TV credits, and to get on TV, you needed credits. You see the problem, right? I begged my agents to get me some auditions and a few came in. I tried out for *30 Rock* and *Boardwalk Empire,* but I wasn't even getting close to booking anything.

Then, one day, I got an audition for *Law & Order: SVU.* It was to be a director. Of child pornography. Classic *SVU.* Was it my dream role? No. But I was in no position to turn down the audition. To my surprise (and horror) I got a callback. The *SVU* callback process is very straightforward: They pick two people for each role and bring you both back at the same time. One by one, you read for the director and producers, and then they make their decision. I was told I would know if I got the role within an hour of my callback. It seemed very civilized.

It was wild to see that waiting room, though. *SVU* always has characters who are in extreme distress. People who have just been beaten, assaulted, raped, tortured. It's a tall order to jump in there and just nail those scenes out of context. Luckily, I just had to be creepy, but other people were working up to full tears. I noticed that the woman next to me was listening to Peter Gabriel's "Don't Give Up" on repeat while wringing her hands and silently weeping. (I really hoped she got the part after all she put herself through.)

I spotted my competition immediately. He was a small redheaded man about my age. In some ways it was easier that we didn't look alike. The casting directors were obviously throwing out a wide net. The redhead went first. He came out looking confident. Then I went in. The directors were all very polite, if not mostly silent. I read the scene, they thanked me and gave a pithy "Very nice work," and I left. The redhead and I walked down the stairs together silently. I thought about saying something to him like "Good luck!" or "Great hair!" but I chickened out. Thirty minutes later, I got the call from my agent that I would not be playing a kiddie-porn director. It was going to the redhead. It was for the best. My mother would have been horrified anyway. But that would be my last TV audition for some time. I just couldn't seem to break into that world.

Years later, after *The Book of Mormon,* the doors to the land of television and film started to open. I was on not one but two TV shows within a year of being in *Mormon,* and got a small role in an indie film called *The Bachelorette.* I thought I was perhaps done auditioning forever! Oh, how wrong I was. The auditions would continue, only now I was competing with a smaller, but arguably more talented and more experienced, group of actors.

One of the first film auditions I had in L.A. was for a remake of *National Lampoon's Vacation.* It was the small part of a whitewater rafting instructor. It didn't feel like a great fit, but they had specifically asked to see me, so I was excited to go in. When I walked into the waiting room, there was one other actor there, Ryan Kwanten. Ryan fucking Kwanten. I don't know if you watched *True Blood* on HBO, but Ryan Kwanten was great on that show as the lovable but dimwitted Jason Stackhouse. Oh, and he's a goddamn smoke show. He has the collective hotness of all the men in an Abercrombie & Fitch catalog and was blessed by the baby Jesus to walk about the Earth creating sunshine and rainbows with his handsomeness and abs.

I was flummoxed. *We can't both be auditioning for the same part. We are barely the same species.* I snuck glances while I pretended to work on my audition scene. I was starting to feel like Sloth from *The Goonies* sitting in the same room with him. He caught me looking. He smiled. If I had any disease or illness in my body, it was instantly healed by the power of that smile. Then he spoke. "It's a funny scene, yeah?" He's Australian, did I forget to mention that? So not only is he like Malibu Ken come to life, he also has the traditionally accepted hottest accent of all time. I stumbled and fumbled and finally said, "You would be really funny in this part." What?! What was I saying? He just smiled, and that concluded our exchange. I did not get that part. Neither did Ryan. But the bigger takeaway from that experience is that I can tell you, with confidence, that Ryan Kwanten smells good.

One of my most mortifying auditions came when I tried out to be an elf in a Christmas movie. I got two call-backs and kind of thought I was nailing it. I was pretty certain that I would be that elf. Finally, I received the feed-back that the director thought that I "didn't seem grounded enough." To play an elf. A fucking elf. I don't think that movie ever came out, so that's fine.

And then there are commercial auditions, which took up a fair amount of time in my early career. This was back when you could make a lot of money for just one commercial. The residuals alone could free you from a day job for a year. All my young actor friends knew this and flocked to every possible commercial audition they could get into.

Let me tell you, they are pretty demoralizing. The casting directors usher you through like cattle. You say whatever line or lines you are supposed to say and then they rush you out. You also have to start the audition with what they call in the biz a slate. You just look directly into the camera and say your name, your height, and who your agent is. It's simple enough, but it is when actors can really lose their minds. For example, some actors, rather than just sticking to the facts of the slate, will add things like, "Well hello there! I'm Andrew Rannells from the great state of Nebraska. I'm six feet two inches on a good day but can shrink to six feet one if it's cold out, and I am represented by the good folks at Catch a Rising Star Management!" Attempts like this are usually met with an eye roll from the casting assistant running the camera.

And it doesn't get better after the slates, as I experienced while auditioning for a Gillette razors commercial. There were six guys about my age all lined up in front of the camera. The casting director bluntly said, "Take off your shirts." I was surprised by this. It was straight out of the movie *Fame*. Everyone did as they were told and then the casting director went down the line, looking us up and down. Much to my horror, she then started saying, apparently in reference to our physiques, "Yes. Yes. No. No. Yes." She got to me. "No." The yeses got to stay and pretend to shave, and the nos had to awkwardly put on their shirts and slink out of the room.

After that humiliation, I made my way to another audition. This one was for Pepsi. At these auditions, you are often given another actor to read with, so you really get to see others' neuroses up close and you can share yours with them. It's a real joy. In this case, I was paired with a man who had the energy of a birthday party magician, but with a competitive darkness that wafted aggressively from him. I asked him if he wanted to read through the scene before we went in and he said, "I'm good." Cool, brah. Way to be collaborative.

We got into the room and he slated first. He came out of the gate HOT. "Hey, friends! I'm Tommy Shoeshine and I am THRILLED to be here. I LOVE Pepsi! And I'm with Tiny Bow Tie Talent Agency." I was sad for him. He was too eager, too pushy. It was my turn. "Hi. I'm Andrew Rannells. . . ." It was at this point, dear reader, that something truly unexpected happened. Tommy Shoeshine, ever so quietly, only loud enough for me to hear him, mocked my slate and repeated, "I'm Andrew Rannells," in a whiny, bratty, tiny voice. But I was the only one who heard it. I was shocked. What the fuck, man?! We are in this together! I lamely finished my slate in total disbelief that this fucking douche was trying to sabotage my audition. We read the scene, I barely tried, and then I ran out of the room, too pissed to even confront Tommy Shoeshine. Once on the street, I called my commercial agent and told them I was done auditioning for a while. I don't think they cared. They had hundreds of other clients who would fill my space.

I never had much luck with commercials, but one area that I was actually successful at was voice-overs. I was a booking machine when it came to commercial voice-overs. I had started doing them as a kid in Omaha, and for whatever reason I just understood how to sell that, how to drop into that place. I give credit to my first acting teacher, Pam Carter. She was the voice-over queen of Omaha, and I learned everything I know about that part of the business from her. Now, this is not to say that I booked every audition—certainly not. My numbers were just much better than my on-camera numbers, which weren't hard to beat. Nothing amazingly glamorous, but they kept me financially afloat. There was one big one that got away, however. My voice-over white whale, if you will. It was a campaign, several spots included, and would be very lucrative. It was to be the voice of an animated butt wipe for Pampers. Specifically, a flamingo that represented the butt wipe. I wanted that job so badly. I needed it. But alas, Pampers chose someone else. That butt wipe was not meant to be mine. It still stings.

I continue to audition frequently today, but things have shifted a bit. There are more offers, and there are more meetings with directors rather than traditional auditions, but there are still plenty of times that I have to roll up my sleeves and bust out that audition charm. I jack my hair up, make sure my forehead isn't shiny, and try to present as open and easy to work with. Mostly these days, directors cast from tape. On one hand, this is great. You get to control the final product, and you can do as many takes as you want until you are happy with it. On the other hand, you have to be your own camera operator, sound engineer, and editor, and you have to find someone to read with you. Roping in friends to do this can be a real pain, but I have enough actor friends that we all just sort of help one another out when needed. I have put Zuzanna through hell recently, getting her to put me on tape for all sorts of weird projects. Just recently I needed her help for an audition for a big-budget sci-fi movie. The scene was absurd, and at one point I had to passionately shout, "But what about the bird flu?!" We had a hard time getting through that one.

So what have I really learned after all these auditions? I don't like auditioning! Who wants to put themselves in a position where you are going to be told no 90 percent of the time? Not this guy! However, when I started to realize that it's ultimately not personal and the best one can do is one's best in that moment, it actually started to get a little easier. Rejection is always hard, but when I am able to remind myself that just like I am not right for every role, not every role is right for me, it does make it a little easier. I said A LITTLE! While the projects might be shinier and the co-stars more famous, the feeling of putting yourself out there is the same as it was when I first started trying out for community theater as a kid. It's the same nerves, the same excitement, the same second-guessing, the same high when you know you've done well, and by far the same low when you are told you didn't get the part. It is just a fact of this business, and not one that will be going anywhere anytime soon. But when it does all come together, when the hard work pays off and the circumstances line up and you are told that you got the job, it's one of the greatest feelings in the world. To get to do the thing that you love to do and get paid for it is a pretty incredible experience.

But you know what? I want to retract something: I'm not always sad when I find out I didn't get a part. When I didn't get the elf part in that Christmas movie, I wasn't sad. I was fucking pissed! Not grounded enough to be an elf . . . I could have been grounded as hell as that elf! Oh well. Their loss.

HORSES,
NOT ZEBRAS

SOMETIMES AT THE BOTTOM OF AN ACTOR'S RÉSUMÉ there is a tiny subsection that says, "Special Skills." If I am being honest, I should always include that my "special skill" is the ability to produce panic in myself in a matter of seconds. I can imagine situations that might never happen in real life and replay them again and again in my head until they seem real to me.

Part of this skill is my background in acting, which allows me to really commit to even the most ridiculous of situations (like when I had to say, quite seriously, in *Pokémon Live!*, "You'll never see Pikachu again!"). And part of it is a special gift, passed down in my DNA—thanks, ancestors!—that allows me to turn any feeling into a completely irrational one at a moment's notice. It's a lingering dread that any good event could be immediately followed by a catastrophe.

This birthright was initially sold to me by my grandmother and mother as a source of humility. *Just because everything is going well, it doesn't mean it couldn't all change in an instant, so be grateful for what you have.* It's made me practical, always plotting my next move and looking around corners for the next problem, any problem, that could pop up. It's a good reminder to not take things for granted, but if pushed too far it just makes you nervous all the time.

I was recently reminded by Zuzanna of something her father taught her about anxiety when she was a child. He told her that there will be times in life when you are scared and anxious, and you may not know how to deal with it or control it, but you shouldn't let your mind drift to the worst possible scenario. Most of the time, the fears we imagine are things that we already know how to handle.

He equated it to being in the woods. You hear the sound of hooves galloping behind you. Not just one set, but several. Louder and louder, closer and closer. *You think, I'm being chased by a dazzle of zebras!** *What to do? Where to go?*

---

* Quick side note: A pack of zebras is called a "dazzle." A dazzle of zebras. Is that not the best thing ever? Not to mention the gayest? I didn't want to just drop that phrase in for fear you would think I was making it up or having a stroke, but now that I have explained it, let's proceed.

Are zebras dangerous? Will they trample me? Can I run? The
sound gets louder and louder, closer and closer. There is no
outrunning them. Finally, with no options, you turn to face
the dazzle of zebras and then you see . . . they're not zebras,
they're horses. They don't harm you, they don't stop, they
just run past. They were never after you, and they were
never dangerous to begin with. And yet, your mind went
straight to the most extreme possibility—being trampled
by the dazzle—filling you with unnecessary fear and anxiety. I loved this advice. It explained so much of what I'd felt
throughout my life.

When I was thirteen, I was in a production of *On Golden
Pond* at the Firehouse Dinner Theater in Omaha, the only
professional theater in the city at that time. It was a big
deal for me and I was the only child in the cast. The actor
playing Ethel (the Katharine Hepburn part) was named
Louise Filbert and she quickly became a second grandmother to me. (Well, technically third, but I never knew
my dad's mom because she died before I was born. So let's
say second.) On opening night, Louise and I were standing
backstage together getting ready to take our bows at the
end of the show, and she took my hand and said, "Remember this. Just like there is an opening night, there will be a
closing night. So take it all in."

I've always remembered that. Every opening night
I have, I almost immediately think of what my closing
will be like. I always thought of this as being practical,

but lately I have realized that fast-forwarding to the closing night on opening night is also a real mind fuck. It
doesn't really make you present; it actually sucks the joy
out of the moment you are in. I'm not saying Louise was
wrong. She was absolutely right; we all should be grateful
for where we are in that exact moment. She was well into
her sixties at this point and was passing this piece of wisdom down to me from a lifetime of experience. But in my
thirteen-year-old brain, I think I got the message wrong,
or at least mixed up. Yes, there will be a closing night, but
that doesn't mean you can't bask in the joy of the opening
night. Fast-forwarding to the end is the exact opposite of
being present.

This idea of emotionally fast-forwarding bled into other
aspects of my life, too. Dating, for example. I rarely start a
relationship without thinking about what the end might be
like. What's our first fight going to be? If he moves in, what
will it be like when he is no longer here? This might be a
chicken-or-the-egg situation, but because I think about
these things early, I have generally had very clean breakups.
*What do I need to get out of here when I leave? My favorite
sweater is in his drawer, so don't forget to grab that.* My bags
are always packed in my head. I don't want to be caught off
guard in the moment. I know what I'll say, the points I'll
make, the feelings I'll share. I want to have the zinger, the
line that he'll never forget. It's a sick, actor-y way of preparing for a moment that may or may not come. I've started

to wonder: Do I manifest these situations by thinking about them? Planning for them? Why can't I stop?

This is when genetics can be both a blessing and a curse. Yes, I inherited my mother's cheekbones, but the Rannells are a tough and tightly wound clan. My dad, Ron, passed on the mental stoicism of my small-business-owner and farmer forefathers, who believed that one must just plow ahead at all times. *Never mind that pain in your back! Take a pill and muscle through! Who cares if you are sad today? Slap on a smile and barrel forward!* Ron was not a "feelings" kind of guy. You swallowed whatever feeling you had and you got the task at hand done.

To be clear, this was not a hard-and-fast rule with Ron. Emotionally, yes. Physically, no. Ron was . . . what's the best way to put this? Kind of a baby when it came to physical ailments. He had a very low pain tolerance and was not afraid to go to the doctor for anything. In this sense, I think we all got a little bit of Ron, because another favorite pastime for the Rannells family is googling physical symptoms. The amount of time we all spend on WebMD is shocking. Except for my brother Dan. I think he has a better relationship with the internet than the rest of us. If you could see my search history over the years, you would be stunned by the number of times I have looked up "I think my teeth are loose. Is that bad?" or "Is dizziness a sign of a brain tumor?" Sometimes when I visit my doctor he says, "What do *you* think you have?" It's his polite way of saying,

"What have you been googling at three A.M., Andy?" I tell myself I am doing this so I am ready for anything. But ultimately, it just makes me spiral.

My mother, Charlotte, on the other hand, gifted me the physical stoicism of my Polish ancestors, who have given her a much stronger constitution. When I was in *Hamilton* on Broadway, Charlotte and my sister Natalie came to see the show. On their way home, at the Newark airport, Charlotte fell getting off an escalator. As Natalie described it, it was a bad fall. Bad enough to make my sweet mother scream out, "OH FUCK!" as she was falling in the middle of Newark airport. Despite whatever pain or embarrassment she might have been feeling at that moment, she got up, walked to her plane, sat for a three-and-a-half-hour flight back to Omaha, and *then* went to the emergency room. It turns out she had broken her damn hip! But she got on the plane anyway. When I asked her about this, she said, "Well, I didn't want to go to an ER in New Jersey." Charlotte Rannells, ladies and gentlemen!

While I have never fallen in an airport, nor have I ever had a fear of that (it might be added to the list later), I have my own Rannells-y anxiety about air travel. The strange thing is that it's relatively new. I was fourteen when I got on a plane for the first time, and I was more excited than scared. The thought of its crashing never really entered my mind. When I moved to New York years later, I only flew home once or twice a year, so my flying was limited and straightforward. I needed to get home to see my family, therefore I had to get on a plane; I didn't really think about it too much. (Full disclosure: Because my trips home were usually Christmas visits, I was often hungover when I flew home. The night before, my friends and I would have been celebrating the end of finals and the beginning of our holiday break. I would roll onto the plane with very little sleep and reeking of gin and tonics. This would ultimately end with my mother picking me up from the airport and immediately proclaiming, "Jesus, Andy. You look like hell." Merry Christmas, Mom. Merry Christmas.)

My worries about flying—at least ones that didn't involve my vomiting up Tanqueray—didn't start until years later, when I began flying with more frequency. I was living in New York but flying to L.A. about once a month for work. As I flew more often, the thought of an accident started to creep in. I guess it was a numbers game at that point. More flying meant a greater possibility that something would go wrong, right? That's just common sense and math. (Two things that I have never gotten high grades in.)

This fear wasn't crippling. I still got on the plane. I didn't have to take a Xanax to do so. I was ultimately fine, but my mind would race. I suddenly became very aware of the other people on the plane. Because the flights were for work, I was being flown by television studios, which would often fly me first-class. The hot towels, the welcome cham-

pagne, the Bose headsets to watch your in-flight movie—
it's all fantastic, and it's even better if you aren't paying for
it yourself. What first class also gives you is a perfect van-
tage point to see which famous people are on your flight.
For me this was a fun pastime, but it also took my mind
down a dark path. Like . . . really dark. I found myself
thinking, *Is that the type of celebrity that would die in a plane
crash?* I don't want to actually name names, because I don't
believe that energy should be put into the universe, but I'd
like to think you understand.

These days, I find myself wondering, *Do I, Andrew Rannells, seem like the type of person who might die in a plane
crash?* Personally, I don't think so. An accident on a state
fair Tilt-A-Whirl? Probably. Falling down an escalator at
the Mall of America? Probably. Choking on a hot dog in a
speed-eating competition? Most likely. But an airplane? I
don't think so. That's not to say that thought hasn't crept
into my head though.

Once, I was flying from L.A. to New York with my *Girls*
co-star Allison Williams, a real gem of a human. We were
on an early-morning flight and I was thrilled to be next to
her. Shortly after taking off, we both opened our books and
were reading quietly like the good little nerds we are, with
blankets on our laps and reading glasses secure on our faces,
when the plane started to drop suddenly. And then rise.
And then drop again. It was very unsettling. I looked for
the flight attendants. They were seated and belted in, and

one had her eyes closed. *Is she praying?* I thought. *That's not a good sign.* The plane dropped and rose a few more times. I heard several passengers let out brief little screams as the plane fell and rose. But it was mostly eerily silent. No message from the cockpit. Nothing.

I started to get scared. *What if I am the type of person who dies in a plane crash? What if that's how it ends for me?* I was frozen in my seat. I wanted to close my eyes like that flight attendant and just pray that this would be over. I looked over at Allison to comfort her, and to have her comfort me. She was still reading her book. She seemed relaxed, calm, still. "This turbulence is wild," I said. She slowly glanced up from her book and then looked me in the eyes from over her chic reading glasses and said, "It'll be fine. Why would *this* be the plane that crashes?" And then she went back to her book. She was right. The plane leveled off, there was no more turbulence, drinks and lunch were served, and Allison and I watched *The Notebook.* After a rocky start, it was a very uneventful trip.

Allison knew sometimes turbulence is turbulence, not a harbinger of horrible things. It's often just part of flying, a few bumps here and there. Sometimes a problem is more straightforward than our narcissistic minds imagine it to be. It doesn't always have to be the worst possible scenario. Just as Zuzanna's dad taught me, sometimes it's just a simple pain in the ass that we know exactly how to deal with.

I think about the zebras every time I start to feel anxious or scared about something. It doesn't mean that the problem doesn't exist or that my concerns aren't valid. It just means that I probably have dealt with something similar in the past, it wasn't catastrophic, and I made it through. That I know how to deal with this.

Lately, I have been trying to make sense of my relationship to anxiety. Not so much its origin but how to cope with it now. I decided the first step was to name it, to humanize this shadowy feeling. I call it "Mr. Anxiety." When he's parceled out, I like Mr. Anxiety. He gives me an edge, a sharpness, that I have come to count on. There have been times in my adult life when I've tried different medications to combat him. They worked for a time—and I know they're lifesavers for many—but honestly, I found I missed him. I missed my edge. I felt too rounded out and often flat.

Mr. Anxiety is like an old friend that I have come to rely on. Okay, maybe not a friend, but a fuck buddy that I have grown comfortable with. But as we all know, or maybe some of us know, a fuck buddy taken too far can become a problem. You can become dependent on that fuck buddy, and they can keep you from moving forward and having meaningful relationships. Or they become clingy and start showing up at your stage door after work, wanting you to take them to dinner and then invite them back to your place for a sleepover. (Maybe that's too specific, but please plug in your own version of "stage door" there.) So I have been trying to figure out how to take the best parts of Mr. Anxiety—the parts that keep me alert, keep me prepared—and let go of the parts that just turn me into a puddle of insecurity.

The older I get, the more I realize I don't think my natural predisposition toward unnecessary worry is going to change anytime soon. All the therapy and self-help books in the world are not going to change my entire personality and forty-plus years of conditioning. But I can try to figure out better ways to deal with it, to train him to be more positive, to be more like Allison Williams. There is no reason that he has to say, "You are probably never going to work again, Andrew. You might want to figure out something else to do with the rest of your life." He could also say, "Hey, Andrew! I think you are nailing it, and you know what? You might be on your way to a CableACE Award soon!"

If Mr. Anxiety is going to be sticking around, he might as well learn some new tricks. And when he does slide back into his old negative patterns, I am reserving the right to occasionally say to him, "Hmmm . . . you might be right about that. It's worth sitting with that for a moment. Do you want to come over?" But I also have the right to say, "Shut up, asshole! I'm trying to enjoy this moment!"

I'm not saying that this is going to cure my current anxiety or the inherent anxiety I got from my ancestors. I still often default to thinking zebras are galloping behind me. But I think it can help me reframe and reintroduce it to my life. Who knows? Maybe Mr. Anxiety can go from fuck buddy to actual friend.

I think it's worth a shot.

THE SCHOOL OF
MUSICAL THEATER

———

'M NOT A PARTICULARLY FAST LEARNER, I HAVE TO BE
honest. Yes, I can pick up a tune pretty quickly, and I have
never met a piece of IKEA furniture that has stumped me,
but life lessons come much slower. The time delay can be
significant sometimes. It's like I'm via satellite.

While I didn't exactly excel in school, there was one
subject I thrived at: musical theater. Okay, maybe that
wasn't part of the official curriculum at Our Lady of
Lourdes—it was more of a vocational class that I created
myself—but I was the top student every year. I also quickly
learned that musical theater can teach a lot about life in
return, if you have teachers like Sondheim, Schwartz, and
Hammerstein. Sometimes these lessons come from just listening to a cast album. Other times, you discover them by

being part of a production, as I did with *Hairspray,* my first Broadway show, my childhood dream come true.

Eight months into my run as Link Larkin, I was visited by one of the show's producers, Margo Lion. She had never stopped by before, so this struck me as odd. She sat down in my dressing room and launched into a speech I'm sure she had given many times before about a show being a living, breathing entity, and how, periodically, new blood (a terrifying way to talk about actors) is needed to keep the show exciting. I could sense where this was going.

I should mention that *Hairspray,* at this point, had become *The Love Boat* in its constant search for "famous" people to bring into the show. It's called "stunt casting" in the biz. If you snag someone who was recently kicked off *American Idol,* ticket sales could go up. It doesn't really matter if they can sing or dance or act as long as they deliver their fans.

My mind started racing as Margo was talking to me. Who was coming in to replace me? One of the brothers from Hanson? A *Survivor* castoff? Let me pause before I recount this next bit to say, for legal purposes, that this is what I *RECALL* she said next. Margo looked at me sweetly and finished twisting the knife in my heart by saying, "We are not going to renew your contract next month. We are bringing in a great young guy from the national tour named Aaron Tveit. You would love him. He's like you but younger and straight." That is what I *RECALL* she said while firing me.

I now know it's illegal to say that (and fucking rude), but at the time I was just overwhelmed. My mind was spinning. I mean, I had known that being replaced might happen one day, but now? I didn't have another job lined up; I didn't have as much saved as I had hoped; I didn't want to leave Tracy Turnblad and the Broadway version of Baltimore. I wanted to stay until I was ready to leave. But the decision had been made. Aaron Tveit was taking my place in this show.

I had really come to love Link Larkin. Yes, he was my first lead on Broadway, so he will always hold a special place in my heart, but he was also a part that I was really good at. I was the right age (twenty-six but a Broadway eighteen), his music fit my voice well, and I could relate to a character who wanted to be a good person but who got caught up chasing a career that seemed like it was within reach. And my hair looked really great in that pompadour! I sort of thought I would just keep doing that show until *I* was ready to leave on my terms. But that's not the way show business or real life works. Most of the time life has its own plans for you and you just have to roll with it.

I started thinking about the two other actors who had played Link Larkin before me on Broadway. And the actors who played him on tour. All the understudies who sometimes played Link and all the actors who would play him in the future. That part didn't belong to any of us.

I left *Hairspray* and went on to do a couple of regional gigs, but nothing came close to my Broadway experience. Six months later I was back in my studio apartment, looking at a bank statement that was aggressively mocking me with my financial reality, when I got a phone call. *Hairspray* was asking me to come back to the show in the ensemble as Fender and *understudy* the role of Link. I needed the job and I needed the money, but I was scared about going back into the ensemble. Was this a big step backward, or just something I needed to do?

My fear of being evicted and having to crawl back to Omaha and live in my mother's basement won out, and I accepted the offer. On one hand it was fun and comfortable, but on the other, it felt strange to be back where I had first started in the show. At that time Ashley Parker Angel of O-Town fame was playing Link Larkin. One night we were onstage about to do "I Can Hear the Bells." There was some downtime for the boys at the top of the scene and our mics were off, so we could talk about whatever. Ashley looked at me and said, "I hear you used to play this part." It kind of took the wind out of me for a moment.

"Yeah, I did," I said sort of sheepishly.

"That's so cool" was his reply.

That's so cool.

It was mine for nine months and then it was time to share it with someone else. Keeping this Link lesson in mind has often come in handy. I continued to replace actors in shows, and I am certain that I will again in the future. Margo was right about one thing: Theater is a living, breathing entity that needs to adapt. That advice has kept me and my often-fragile ego in check.

When I was first cast in *Jersey Boys,* there were five Bob Gaudios playing the role eight times a week all over the world. And that's not counting the real Bob Gaudio, who was just walking around as a real-life human every second of the year. This cloning of Bob Gaudios eventually led to a very toxic game that was played where most toxic games are played: the internet. Fans of *Jersey Boys* loved to compare us and would often Frankenstein us together to make one complete "Dream Bob." "If *he* looked like *him* but sounded like *him* but acted like *him* and had *his* hair, that would be the perfect Bob." Usually I lent the hair to Dream Bob, which was not the ideal contribution when ranking talents.

Patti LuPone, all-around goddess and, in my mind, my best friend—sorry, Zuzanna—talked about this in her book, *Patti LuPone: A Memoir.* This game of comparing and contrasting actors in the same role might be fun for the audience, but it is not fun when you are playing the part. You are trying to make it your own, to put your own spin on it, and often the little changes you implement anger people. Everyone seems to want what they saw first, and that standard becomes an unfair bar for other actors to reach in the same role.

I experienced this phenomenon again when I replaced Neil Patrick Harris in *Hedwig and the Angry Inch* and Jonathan Groff in *Hamilton*. (Though with Jonathan it was a little different. At the time he was on *Looking* and I was on *Girls*, and a lot of the audience just thought, *Oh! It's that white gay guy from HBO!* and I got a pass.) There was just no avoiding the comparisons.

I learned this lesson from a different perspective after I left *The Book of Mormon*. I felt great ownership of Elder Price. I had helped bring him into existence, and I felt my fingerprints all over his short-sleeved white dress shirt. But then it was time for me to leave the show and I had to pass his Mormon name tag on to someone else. Luckily, I got to give it to my friend Matt Doyle and I knew Elder Price was in good hands. Later, it went to Gavin Creel, and then to my standby Nic Rouleau, who has played the part longer than anyone, and on and on. It wasn't my role to begin with. I am part of a legacy of Prices, in a line of actors who keep that show going.

I often think of something that Stephen Bogardus, the original Whizzer in *Falsettos*, said to me at the opening night of the show's revival in 2016. He pulled me aside at the party afterward and said, "I am really happy to see Whizzer on Broadway again. I am happy you get to know him, too." It was extremely generous of him to say that, especially considering I grew up listening to Stephen sing that score and I had his voice in my head every night onstage. He also knew that these great roles were meant to be shared.

I am certain there is a proverb or an old poem or quote from a great thinker that could have taught me this much earlier in my life had I been paying closer attention. I could have saved myself a lot of stress had I studied more in school, I suppose. But I had to learn this much the same way I learned a lot of things: through musical theater. (The same way I learned who shot William McKinley, who Georges Seurat was, and how many minutes are in a year. Let that be a lesson to our government, which keeps cutting arts funding! You can pass a whole bunch of history tests by listening to *Assassins, Sunday in the Park with George,* and *Rent!*)

Like a lot of other lessons I have learned in the theater, "The part doesn't belong to you" translates to life offstage, too. For a long time, when I ran into someone I had dated, especially men I'd had a serious relationship with, I would think, *There's my ex-boyfriend.* I still felt an ownership of some kind. But at some point, I saw one of them and had to remind myself, *Rannells! That is not your ex-boyfriend. That is someone else's current boyfriend (and in some cases, husband). He's not yours anymore.* That's not *my* old apartment, that's someone else's home.

I think it's helped me to be less precious, maybe. To realize that everything is in motion and we just have to keep adapting, too. I find it comforting that we are all a part of this cast of characters that make up the world, and our roles are always changing. Sometimes we are the lead, sometimes we're in the chorus; often we are stage managers, and a lot of times we are the audience, bearing witness to what's happening around us. But we are always a part of the production.

THE BOOK THAT
CHANGED MY LIFE

I DON'T KNOW FOR CERTAIN, BECAUSE I HAVE NEVER administered a formal poll of the population, but I think most people can easily pinpoint the moment that their life changed forever. Some folks would say it's the moment they first saw their child, or perhaps met their spouse. Of course, tragedy also causes profound changes in people, which is horrifically sad, but I am thinking about a different kind of change. A moment that brings clarity and purpose to one's life. For me, I can tell you the exact moment my life changed forever. It began with *The Book of Mormon*.

No, not the Book of Mormon that Joseph Smith dictated while staring into a top hat filled with magic stones. (Look it up. That's true.) It was the *Book of Mormon* that was presented to me by Trey Parker, Matt Stone, and Bobby Lopez. I know a musical comedy may not seem as important as having a baby or getting married, but this show was a version of my baby *and* my husband all wrapped up in one two-and-a-half-hour Broadway show.

It all started as I was doing a production of *Smokey Joe's Cafe* at the Paper Mill Playhouse. (You might be familiar with that show as one of your grandparents' favorite musicals.) With two weeks left in the run, my agent called me with an exciting audition. It was to play a nineteen-year-old Mormon missionary for the workshop of *The Book of Mormon.* Very little information was being shared, and auditioners were asked to sing their own material and be prepared to cold-read scenes if needed. I accepted the audition immediately.

One of my *Smokey Joe's* castmates, Maia Wilson, had done the last reading of *The Book of Mormon.* I went to her dressing room and asked her about the show. I wanted to hear more about the actual story, and I was concerned that the character was supposed to be nineteen years old. Could I even pull that off? Maia has a calm wisdom to her. Like she knows things no one else knows. She looked at me for a long time and then said, "This is your gig. You are going to get this part."

"What about the nineteen-years-old thing? I'm thirty-one."

She laughed. "They don't know you! *Just be nineteen.* Go get your job!"

She was right. They didn't know me. I was an unknown

guy coming in to meet them for the first time. I could be whoever they wanted.

The audition process felt like any other I had experienced, except that they wouldn't let you leave with any of the audition material. They even took your phone so you couldn't take pictures of your audition sides. You had to come early, take a quick look at the scenes, and then just sort of wing it.

I had been auditioning for years at this point and had read a lot of scripts. Some were very good and some were . . . not so good. I usually found myself looking for problems in scenes, looking for questions. It's difficult to prepare audition material when the scenes aren't great, but in the case of *The Book of Mormon,* the second I read those scenes I had a very clear thought: *You know exactly how to do this.*

It seemed obvious what to do to become Elder Price. I understood him and his quest for missionary greatness, in part, because I felt like I *was* him. No, I had never been a missionary and I was not religious, but I knew that feeling he had, that drive to be the best and succeed at all costs. I just had to substitute musical theater for Mormonism and Stephen Sondheim for Joseph Smith, and all of a sudden I knew what to do. I wasn't nervous, I wasn't overwhelmed, I just felt like everything I had worked toward in the past, all my other auditions, had led me to this moment. That sounds very lofty and somewhat spiritual, but it's true. And I also knew that even if they didn't cast me, I had walked into that room and poured my heart and guts out. There was nothing else I could have done. They would either agree with me that I was the Elder Price they had been searching for, or they wouldn't.

Thankfully, they agreed with me. Within a few weeks I was in a rehearsal studio with the cast of what would become *The Book of Mormon*. I should mention that I was the only new principal, or leading character, that they added for their final workshop before Broadway. The show had replaced every Elder Price they had worked with up until this point. They had done two readings and one workshop, and every time a different actor had worn Elder Price's missionary name tag. The show wasn't officially slated to come to Broadway just yet. This would be the final push to secure their funding to make that move. What's more, no one in the cast had a contract for Broadway. They could still make cast changes if they wanted to. Would I be the Price they kept? Or would I be replaced as well, like the Prices before me? This workshop was essentially an extended audition for all of us, but particularly for me.

I'm going to be totally honest with you, and this is not something I have shared with a lot of people: Knowing that they had never stuck with the same Elder Price twice, I made a tactical decision to leave my mark on this workshop. If I was only here for this moment, I might as well tailor this music to my voice and my particular style of singing. So all the songs became just a bit higher. That's where I was most comfortable. Did the thought cross my mind, *This could potentially make it harder for other tenors to sing?* Yes, yes it did. I knew there were other people who could sing it, but I was the only one in front of the creative team. I remember Stephen Oremus, the musical director, saying to me, "Are you sure you want to sing it up there?" To which I always replied, "Yes." I was going to make this *my* part. At least for now.

Trey Parker and Matt Stone were also very generous with me when it came to the writing of Elder Price. We had similar senses of humor, and they allowed not just me but the whole cast to have input as to how the dialogue flowed. Josh Gad, Nikki James, Rory O'Malley, Michael Potts, and I all got to shape those scenes so they felt right to us. Trey and Matt aren't precious, and they are always trying to make their work better. It's a rare experience to work with writers who give you that space and that control. They knew what they were going for, but in the process they listened to us and valued our input.

Also wildly generous was the cast. Nikki James and I had known each other for many years at this point but had never worked together. I immediately knew that we were going to be friends. She is an amazing talent but also a fierce advocate for herself in the rehearsal room and an incredibly intelligent human. We have a similar work ethic and go very hard when up on our feet shaping or working on a scene, but during breaks in the day, we tend to retreat alone. I spent many a lunch break sitting silently near her, knowing that we both were resting up and focusing on when we had to start creating again. I felt an instant kinship.

Josh Gad, on the other hand, is a force of nature at all times. He can make anything funny, and usually in a most unexpected and brilliant way. But he's not a bulldozer of an actor. He doesn't plow over his co-stars in scenes; he knows when to throw the focus on someone else. I learned with Josh that he and I did not run in the same lane. Our skill sets were very different and we complemented each other perfectly. Josh could be like a tornado, spinning jokes and comedic chaos at any given moment. All I had to do was stand still in his wake and we both got the laughs we were hoping for.

Early on in the workshop rehearsals, we had to do a run-through of the show with a full band and an audience of producers watching. We were all seated because we hadn't started staging anything yet. Trey, Matt, and Bobby just wanted to hear it all. It was the first time the entire cast would hear me sing songs and do scenes that they had seen other actors do many times. I was very nervous, not so much for the producers to render their verdict, but for the cast to see and hear me as Elder Price. Could I impress them? Actors are a fickle bunch, and I include myself in that statement. We can be wildly supportive team players, but we can also be judgy little jerks. Would the cast ultimately accept me as their new Elder Price?

Just a few songs into the first act, we got to my first solo, "Something Incredible," which would later become "You and Me (but Mostly Me)." The song maps out Elder Price's hopes for his future as a missionary in Uganda and is an affirmation to himself that he can do something incredible. Singing that song for all those people for the first time, I got emotional. I wasn't just playing Elder Price, I was telling that room that I was up to this challenge. That I would not let them down and they could all count on me to help make this show a success. While performing, I felt simultaneously very much in my body and in control, but also that I was floating above myself somehow. To quote a lyric from the show, *This was the moment I was born to do.*

I finished the song, and during the applause I locked eyes with Nikki James. She gave me a small smile and a supportive and meaningful wink. I knew I had proven myself and won them over.

The rest of the workshop was a lot of hard but joyful work. I was only focused on that show, day and night, for the four weeks we were all together. Our rehearsals culminated in two presentations for some influential audiences. For me, the most important audience member was Stephen Sondheim. He was friends with Trey, Matt, and Bobby, and had agreed to watch our performance and share his thoughts. I had to push all my nerves aside and try my best to forget he was there, but I was never unaware that I was performing for an icon, a genius, and the artist who had made me want to be an actor in the first place. After the opening number I realized I had been singing so hard that I'd split my bottom lip open. One of my castmates, Brian Sears, said to me before my next entrance, "Dude, you have blood on your chin." I took that as a sign that I needed to relax into this performance. There was still a lot of show left, and I didn't want to be bloody for Mr. Sondheim.

After that workshop, the path to Broadway was cleared and we all got our offers to join the cast. I said yes immediately, but not everyone came back. Not because they were fired, but because they chose not to continue. A couple of people didn't like the material—it was too dark, too offensive. I was really impressed with their ability to say no to this show. I truly respect those folks and their commitment to their principles. (I don't know what it says about me that I didn't bat an eye at lyrics about magical fuck frogs and maggots in scrotums.) Those of us who did say yes would start rehearsals for a full-scale production in January, begin previews in February, and open the show on Broadway on March 24, 2011. This was happening.

The wildest part about being in the show at that time was the secrecy around it. No one outside of the theater really knew what we were up to. There was a lot of chatter about what the show was. The producers kept a tight lid on everything so that when we actually started performing in front of a live paying audience, they had no idea what they were about to see. We were the musical "the *South Park* guys" had written, but no one knew anything else. It's the best way to open a new show, in my opinion. We were able to surprise people and exceed their limited expectations.

Previews were teaching us that we were part of something special, something Broadway had never seen before. Our creative team never stopped working to make the show the best it could be. We were constantly getting changes and learning new material, which was exhausting but mostly exhilarating. I remember Trey, Bobby, and Stephen Oremus teaching me the opening of "Spooky Mormon Hell Dream" in my dressing room during intermission and then putting it into the show moments later in front of a live audience. I felt electric, I felt alive, I felt an overwhelming passion for singing about a maple glazed donut. (If you know the show, you know what I am talking about.)

Four weeks of intense previews finally led to the night we had all been waiting for: opening night. My sister Natalie and my mom flew in from Omaha to be there. They bought fancy new dresses and I hired a hair-and-makeup artist to get them ready for the evening. We had a chauffeur to take us to the party after the show. It was poised to be a very exciting evening. I just had to *do* the show first.

While I was comfortable with the show, and Elder Price

and I had temporarily fused into the same person, opening nights are a whole other experience. The nerves, the excitement, and the potential for failure or mistakes are all jacked up to an eleven on one's personal energy meter. I'd like to be able to tell you some moments I remember from that particular performance. An anecdote that beautifully sums up the experience. But I remember nothing. It happened, I can tell you that. There are photos to prove it! There is a review in *The New York Times*! But I don't remember a goddamn thing. It was too much excitement, too much adrenaline, for the evening. What I *do* remember is being packed in my tiny dressing room with my mom, Natalie, and Zuzanna as we popped a bottle of champagne and toasted to the first night of what would become a long and successful run. They all looked beautiful, and we all cried a bit through smiles of joy. I remember how happy I was that they were there and that all the years of struggle and disappointment in my career had melted away for that moment.

And then there was the party. My first Broadway opening-night soiree. Here's what no one tells you about an opening-night party for a show that you are starring in: You don't get to party. It's an extension of your job. An exciting extension, but still part of your job. We arrived at a huge space called Gotham Hall and I was immediately pulled away from my mom, Natalie, and Zuzanna and thrown into a press room packed with photographers and reporters. I had never experienced anything like it before and I was not prepared. Luckily, I had by my side my first publicist, Mandi Warren, whom I had only met weeks earlier. She was the coolest, calmest, most supportive person I could have asked for at that moment. She guided me through that room seamlessly and always knew just when to pull me away from a reporter and place me in front of a new photographer. I was in a wind tunnel of shouted questions and flashbulbs and barely had time to think about what I was saying. I had been in there for about an hour when Mandi told me that we had done enough for the evening and that I should go find my mom and enjoy the rest of the night.

Before I could get into the main room of the party, my agent stopped me and told me the reviews were in. Thanks to the internet, that stuff gets published while you are still at your opening-night party, for better or worse. In this case, it was for the better, because we were universally hailed as a hit. One performance in and we were already a success. Now we just had to keep doing the show eight times a week at that level. It was instantly daunting, but I set that thought aside for another time. I had to find my opening-night dates somewhere in that huge crush of people who were now celebrating not only the show but also its critical reception. Hundreds of people who'd had no idea who I was only hours before were now congratulating me and asking to take photos with me.

It was overwhelming to walk out of that press room a

different person than the one who had walked in. I was most certainly the same Andrew Rannells, but now all these people knew that I was Andrew Rannells. It was exciting but mostly intimidating. And a bit lonely. I was surrounded by people, but no one I knew. I couldn't find Josh, I couldn't find Nikki, and most important, I couldn't find my mother. I started to get worried that she and Natalie had somehow gotten lost in all this celebration. Where could they be? How would I find them? Zuzanna had my phone in her purse (I didn't want to spoil the line of my suit coat. Fashion before function!), so I couldn't call or text anyone. I was just going to have to circle that room until I spotted them.

Boy, did I spot them. My mom, Natalie, and Zuzanna were standing in a clump, all holding champagne flutes and laughing and looking incredibly happy. My mom's face was lit up in a way I had never seen before. I recognized her as Charlotte, my mother, but she looked different, younger, at ease in a way I hadn't witnessed before in my whole life. There was someone else in this circle, someone with his back to me who I couldn't make out. *Who are they talking to?* I got closer and saw that it was Paul Rudd. Paul fucking Rudd! I had admired him for years, and here he was cutting up with Charlotte, Natalie, and Zuzanna! Natalie spotted me as I got closer, and they all hugged and congratulated me again. Zuzanna handed me some champagne and then Mr. Rudd introduced himself. "Hey! I'm Paul! Congratulations, man. You are incredible. It's so great to meet your family. I know that these nights can be a little hectic, so I thought I would keep an eye on your ladies while you did your press rounds."

Are you kidding me? Keep an eye on my ladies? What a fucking gentleman! He had been chatting them all up, keeping their flutes full of champagne and making sure they all felt welcomed and comfortable while I was busy doing press stuff. He didn't even know me, but he was still looking out for me. There is a reason he is known as the nicest man in Hollywood. I think his departure from the group outweighed my arrival, because Charlotte seemed genuinely sad to see him go. She still talks about that night and her brief but meaningful connection with Paul Rudd to this day.

We didn't stay terribly long at the party after that. A few more toasts and then I had to get to bed. We all had to do the show four more times that week before a day off. That's another thing no one tells you about opening a Broadway show: You don't get to rest. You are immediately on that performance train, and it's not stopping.

Here's what I do remember in a major way about that night. As I lay in bed, still too excited to fall asleep and replaying the whole day in my head, I found myself trying to hold on to that feeling, trying to bank all that excitement and joy I had felt. But I was mostly thinking, *Here we go. You are really doing it now, Rannells.* There had been a shift, a swell of growth in my heart, and I knew that things weren't ever going to feel quite the same again. Even if it all went away in the morning, that night had happened. These events existed in my life now. I would be linked to this show, this role, for the rest of my career.

And then, my friends, my ol' pal panic started tapping me on the shoulder. *Things aren't ever going to feel the same again. What does that actually mean? Do I have to be different now? Will people treat me differently?* I didn't really want to change. Of course I wanted more professional opportunities, but I still wanted to be me. I started to feel anxious. My previous excitement turned into a trickle of foreboding. Would anything ever feel this exciting again?

I told myself that I had to shake that off, that I was getting ahead of myself. Everything was great at this moment. I needed to focus on what I knew was true, that tomorrow I would wake up and I would go to the Eugene O'Neill Theatre and I would become Elder Price once again. That was my job for the moment. My anxiety would just have to wait.

RESPECT THY ELDERS

———

ONE OF THE BIGGEST TAKEAWAYS I LEARNED FROM twelve years of Catholic school is the importance of gratitude. You are taught to always be aware of what you have and to thank God for allowing you to have it. That, in and of itself, is not a bad message, depending on your feelings about God. It is important to be grateful for all sorts of things in our lives. Acknowledging them makes it harder to take them for granted. The twist that the Catholics also teach is that you probably don't deserve anything good in the first place.

Never have I felt this internal conflict more than in the summer of 2010. I had just been cast as one of the leads in *The Book of Mormon*. It was a dream come true. And even though we hadn't started rehearsals yet, I could tell that it had the potential to be successful on Broadway. Years of hard work and close calls for other big jobs had finally paid off, and I was going to open my first Broadway show as an original cast member.

I was cast in June and rehearsals wouldn't start until August, so I was in that magical space where I could actually relax into my free time because I had a job coming up. I was trying to prepare for *The Book of Mormon* by working out and singing every day, meeting actual Mormon missionaries, and reading the actual Book of Mormon (she's a slow read; I can't say I recommend her). But I was still left with a lot of downtime. I realized that many people had helped me on my way to *Mormon*, so I decided I should do something helpful for someone else. I had a good idea of what I wanted to do, too.

When I was a kid, I only had one living grandparent: my grandma Josephine. I was very close with her, and her death affected me deeply. I've always had a place in my heart for older people and it only grew after she died. I thought of her every time I ran into an older neighbor in New York, who would often be sitting on the stoop outside her building. Sometimes she would be reading, sometimes she would be talking to another neighbor, but mostly she was alone. I'd say hello when I passed her but I'd never really stop to talk. One day I decided to make a little more time for her. When I asked her how she was doing, she smiled sort of sadly and said, "No one really smiles at me anymore. People just walk by like I'm not here. They used to smile." This broke my heart, the idea that she felt like an invisible person in this city of millions. In addition to taking more time out of my day to talk to this neighbor, I knew I wanted to help more people like her. If I could help someone else feel seen, that seemed like a good use of my free time.

Eventually, I connected with SAGE, an organization that assists older queer folks across the country. They offer many services in New York City, and maybe most important, they also host daily events at the Lesbian, Gay, Bisexual, and Transgender Community Center in the West Village to promote a sense of community. A lot of the folks they reach out to don't have people close to them, and SAGE understands that getting people out of their apartments, talking to others, and hopefully feeling less isolated is crucial for their overall health. SAGE specifically has a program where they pair a younger volunteer with an older participant. These people are often homebound, or leaving their homes is difficult, so you go to them. You might run errands, pick up prescriptions, or just sit with them and talk.

When I inquired about this program, they didn't have anyone in need of a buddy, so I started volunteering at the community center during their weekly coffee klatches. I would come in, make some coffee, put some snacks out, and then just talk to folks. I really enjoyed spending time with them. As they shared their stories of moving to the city decades earlier, they reminded me of my first years in New York. The big difference was that a lot of these people had to leave home because they were queer. They were rejected by their families and communities and had to start over in a place that was more accepting. But even New York was not the most welcoming place. I knew the stories of pre-Stonewall Manhattan, but hearing them firsthand was something altogether different. The brutality, the discrimination, the shame—it was heartbreaking to hear about. But there were also triumphs and love and fun and laughter.

After a few weeks of drinking coffee and gabbing, I was asked to fill in as a home visitor for a volunteer who was going to be out of town for a couple of weeks. He regularly visited two different older gay gentlemen who were unable to leave their apartments, so I was going to pop in and chat with them for a couple of afternoons. I was excited but also a little nervous. I was going to be in their homes, trying to entertain them on some level. What if they didn't like me? What if they thought I was boring? What if my "midwestern charm" didn't work?

The first man I visited—we'll call him Fred—had requested some help with his computer. He had just gotten his first email address and wanted me to walk him through the basics of computer usage. Now, I have never been technologically savvy. I can still be easily brought to tears while trying to navigate Dropbox files, but at the time, I figured

I could be helpful with beginner email jargon. I met Fred at his apartment on the Upper West Side. Fred was in his midseventies, I would guess, and had a constant smile on his face.

"Are you my boy?" he said as he answered the door.

"I am indeed your boy!" I said, probably too chipper, and he welcomed me inside.

His small apartment was filled with books and photos and layered area rugs far older than me. Fred offered me a glass of water and we sat down at the computer to get started. It became immediately clear that Fred did not need help with his email. He seemed very equipped to navigate Gmail and sat patiently as I talked through the basics. He nodded, pretended to "learn" things, and feigned surprise when I told him about cc'ing people, but I could tell I wasn't teaching him anything.

Finally I asked, "Fred, is there something specific you want to do on your computer? You seem like you got this email thing down."

Fred looked a little embarrassed. "Actually yes. Do you think you could help me find someone? Someone specific." Jackpot! Fred was probably trying to track down an old love, maybe an army buddy or a boarding school lover that he hadn't seen in decades, and he wanted to rekindle his romance with him! Maybe they both had been married to women and were now widowed and in a place to be honest about their feelings for each other. Maybe I could help two men find a loving relationship in their twilight years. This was great! I am very good at internet sleuthing. I would find Fred's lost love!

"Yes, Fred! I can totally do that," I said. "Let's go to Google and get cracking! What's his name?"

Fred again looked embarrassed. "I only know his first name: Brandon."

Hmmm . . . Brandon didn't sound like the name of a seventysomething former army buddy, but okay. I could work with this. "What else do you know about Brandon? Where does he live? What city?"

"Oh, he lives here in New York."

"Great. Where does he work? Or does he work here in the city, too?"

"Ummm, yes. He works at the Monster. He's a bartender."

The Monster is one of the oldest gay bars in New York. Generally speaking, it caters to a more mature crowd, and they often have dancers and shirtless bartenders serving drinks. Fred's agenda was becoming clearer. He had a crush. He had a crush on a probably younger, almost certainly shirtless bartender, and he wanted to track him down. I looked up the Monster's website, and right there on the homepage was a series of photos of bartenders and patrons and go-go boys having a gay old time. "Are any of these Brandon?" I asked. Fred scrolled through the photos.

"Yes! That's him! That's Brandon! How did you find him?"

"Well, this is just the bar's website. Let's see if we can find his name."

Sure enough, captioned below the photos was Brandon's name, but not his last name. Fred looked hopeful. Here is when I briefly wrestled with the moral implications of Fred's request. He wanted to track down his favorite bartender online in hopes of contacting him. I didn't know Brandon. I didn't know his life, whether he was gay or straight or in a relationship, or if he would appreciate some bar patron reaching out to him. And for what? To ask him out? To just talk? Maybe I should just encourage Fred to talk to Brandon in person the next time he was at the Monster. Maybe I should protect Brandon and his privacy and cut this off now. But I looked at Fred, so full of hope at this very basic internet search, and I knew I couldn't fail him. I was his SAGE buddy! I was there to help him with whatever he needed, even if that included tracking down on the internet a young man who had served him drinks. "Do you think we can find a way to talk to him?" Fred asked. I paused. I thought about it. And then I said, "Hell yes, Fred! Let's find him!"

I went to Facebook to see if the Monster had a page. Sure enough, they did. And there were even more photos of Brandon there. Mostly shirtless ones. Fred had good taste. It didn't take long to find Brandon's own Facebook page.

"Here he is, Fred."

"Oh wow. What do I do now?" he asked.

"You send him a message! Tell him hello and ask to be his friend on here."

Fred followed my instructions. He sent a very formal message saying hello and that he hoped to see him at the bar soon. It seemed harmless enough and I doubt Brandon responded, but it made Fred very happy. I left him that day with the possibility of some fun and some hope that he had connected with someone. He might have ended up stalking and murdering Brandon, but I think I would have heard about that in the news.

My next assignment was Daryl. Daryl was the same age as Fred and also lived in a large apartment building on the Upper West Side. He was also in need of technical help with his computer. I was assuming it was going to be email or googling something, but Daryl surprised me.

"I'm looking for porn," he told me flatly.

Now, I realize as I write this that it sounds a little nefarious. Like Daryl was using this as a creepy tactic or come-on. But when I tell you it was transactional—it was a function, a necessity—it really was. He wasn't creepy at all, he was just direct. He had sexual needs, just like anyone else. I didn't know exactly how to respond, but again, I wanted to be helpful, so I asked him, "Well . . . what kind are you looking for? We can literally find anything on the internet."

"What do you mean?" he asked.

"For instance, if I type 'gay, big dick, jock porn' into Google, here's what comes up." I showed him. His face lit up.

"That's all I have to do?!"

"Yeah. Just type what you are looking for and then type 'porn' after it. That's all you have to do!"

I had only been in the apartment for ten minutes, but I could tell he wanted me to leave immediately. He had gotten what he wanted. But then he asked, "Are you good with TVs?"

"Sure!" I said. He told me he couldn't get his DVD player to work. I could see that it was on and that a DVD was playing, but it wasn't showing up on the television. "I think you just have to switch the HDMI input on your remote." I showed him how to do it and immediately a gay porn started playing on the TV. Two nineties-looking hunks were going at it in a barnyard. Daryl was mortified and dove for the remote.

"Oh, Daryl. I think we are friends at this point," I said. "We're good."

I made sure he didn't need anything else, like maybe a trip to the pharmacy or a mailbox, but no. Just the porn!

And then I left feeling like I had helped. Was it what I had been expecting? No. I thought it might be more of a grandparent/grandson situation, like the friendship I'd had with Josephine. Even though she was my grandma, I came to think of her as a friend. I thought my tasks with SAGE would be more like going grocery shopping or taking someone to the doctor, but this was important, too. Even though we were separated by decades in age, we were part of the same community of gay men.

I never saw Fred and Daryl again, but I've thought about them a lot. I wonder if Brandon responded. I wonder if Daryl found the porn he was looking for. The truth is, I knew very little about these men other than what I learned in our brief time together. Did they have partners at one point? What was their coming out like? How did they remember the AIDS crisis in New York City? I don't know, and I wish I had asked more questions. I also wondered if that would be my path as an older gay man. Would I still be crushing on bartenders at seventy-five? Would I still be watching porn and jerking off in the afternoon? Probably. And that made me happy.

I mean, there's something sort of sad about the relentlessness of life. That things change but nothing really changes. But there is stability in that also. I want to grow and I want to mature in some ways, but I don't want my personality or my sense of humor or my sexual needs to change. Fred and Daryl showed me that they don't have to. You can still be yourself even if your body switches into a different gear. There's something sweet about that.

Hopefully there will be some young gay who will help me find porn on whatever the internet becomes in thirty years. And hopefully there will always be someone to smile at me on the street. Next time you are walking down the street and you see an older person, do me a favor—and do yourself a favor—and give them a smile. One time I had a woman call me a "fucking creep," but I swear that is not the usual response.

HAVING IT ALL

———

DOES ANYONE *REALLY* NEED A BOYFRIEND? AFTER a few failed attempts over the years, I'm on the fence about this question. I have sex. I have dates. I've had relationships, but none that got in the way of my professional goals. For most of my life, if I've been forced to choose between a career and a love life, I've chosen a career. I have my friends and family and work. Maybe there isn't room for everything. Sometimes I console myself by telling myself that I'm not good at dating anyway. That I don't deserve a boyfriend because I am bad at keeping them.

Now, you may be thinking, as I am thinking as I write this, *Hey, Andrew! Maybe you just picked the wrong people. Maybe you should find someone outside of the business you are in, someone less competitive, someone supportive. Why do you have to be so hard on yourself, Tiger?* (Sometimes I call myself Tiger.) Well, readers, I have a hard time remembering that. Once a pattern is set in our heads, it can be real hard to break. By the time I was in my late twenties, I figured that my pattern, what I had "learned," was that I liked having a boyfriend but wasn't good at relationships. Or maybe I just wasn't ready for a relationship? Maybe I just needed to take a moment and focus on myself. The right guy would appear when I was ready. Right?

Then I met Denis. In my mind, Denis was the answer to my relationship woes and was going to fix everything for me. He was a talented, handsome, incredibly funny, very charming, sensitive man with one minor flaw, or complication: a boyfriend by the name of Matthew, who was also a talented, handsome, incredibly funny, very charming, sensitive man. So I decided that, instead of realizing this fantasy of dating him, I would just be his friend. Maybe the crush I had developed would go away once I truly got to know him.

My first acting teacher, Pam Carter, taught me a very valuable lesson that I would like to pass along to you. If you have a crush on someone, an all-consuming, can't-stop-thinking-about-them-day-or-night, wondering-what-your-wedding-might-be-like crush, try this: The next time you are with them, play a little game in your mind. Pretend that they are already your boyfriend or girlfriend. Take in their whole personality, all their quirks and tics, and imagine that you have to live with them all the time. You have to own their behavior because they are your partner. It's suddenly not so cute that they use crystal deodorant. Those *Black Mirror* references aren't as funny as they think they are. The fact that they say things like "Ibiza is my version of heaven" is now a goddamn nightmare. This trick is a real crush-killer and time-saver. I'm grateful to Pam every time I use it.

The exception proves the rule, and with Denis, Pam's rule made things worse. Denis was everything I thought I wanted and needed. I had to keep reminding myself that he wasn't my boyfriend, he was just my friend. But our friendship spiraled into something that was fraught and often painful, and it involved weepy conversations about our potential and maybe unlikely future. There was kissing in shadows and groping in the back of cabs, but never any sex. That was the one line we didn't cross. It's a cringeworthy time to look back on. Taking responsibility for my own actions, I can say I was foolish, I was naïve, and I was selfish.

I got a job on the national tour of *Jersey Boys* as Bob Gaudio and would be out of town for a year. I told Denis that this was a good opportunity for us to reset. "Let's not speak for a while. You have things to figure out, I have things to figure out. Let's give it some space." So we didn't talk. We didn't text. We didn't email. Things became clearer in my mind. I had real feelings for Denis, but I also knew that carrying on with someone who was supposed to be in a relationship with someone else was a waste of time. He was basically telling me, "Hey! I'm a real shitty boyfriend, FYI!" I thought I was special, but I knew I wasn't *that* special. If he was willing to do this with me, he was probably doing it with someone else, too. It broke me of my crush.

And then . . . he called.

Denis left me a message saying that he and Matthew had broken up. (I would find out later that Matthew broke up with him, but I didn't ask for specifics at the time.) He said he had been thinking about me and missed me and he wanted to be with me if I still wanted to be with him. Any clarity I had gained about him was instantly muddied. Of course I wanted to be with him! In that moment, I wanted to be with him more than anything in the world! So we were together. I felt I had won something. I had won the role of Denis's boyfriend.

We quickly created a great life together. After less than a year of dating, Denis asked me to move in with him. I did, and our relationship seemed better than ever. But professionally, we were both feeling a little stuck. I was doing a lot of readings of new shows, some of which got out-of-town tryouts to move to Broadway, but nothing was certain. Denis was also trying to land an original show as a choreographer and was hoping to get one of the many projects he was developing to Broadway. We were in the same place. We understood each other's goals and dreams, and there is something reassuring and beautiful about that. Something that should have made me feel safe in that moment of professional uncertainty. But my anxiety about my future as an actor got the best of me.

I was finishing a show called *Lysistrata Jones* in Dallas, and the producers hoped it would move to New York. At the time, the chances were looking slim and I was going to need a new job. Denis was about to choreograph a production of *Smokey Joe's Cafe* at the Paper Mill Playhouse in New Jersey. There is one role in that show commonly referred to as "the White Boy Track" that I knew I could do in my sleep. It was only a couple of solos and a lot of backup for others. I asked Denis about it. Since I wasn't in town for the auditions, I suggested that I make a video audition. I was hoping that my two Broadway credits would help me get a leg up on the competition.

Denis was—what's the best way to say this?—less than helpful in assisting me. He said that the director really wanted to see everyone in person and that he wasn't sure a tape would be effective. I tried to control my rage. What good is sleeping with the choreographer if he can't even get you a job!? I knew what was happening, though. Denis didn't want to play favorites, especially for his boyfriend, and I knew that he was making the correct move. *I will get this job on my own, damn it,* I told myself. I made a taped audition where I sang my little heart out and I hoped for the best. To my relief, Paper Mill responded favorably, but they wanted to hear me sing more. So another tape was made. And another. After three auditions I got the job at the Paper Mill. I was relieved, and grateful that I did it without Denis's help.

Smokey Joe's turned out to be more fun than I'd expected, and I really loved working with Denis. Even on a show like that, which is light on substance, he took a lot of care to make sure we all felt good about what we were doing. It was a big reason I was attracted to him in the first place. Once we were open, the run of the show was pretty fast. I think it was only six weeks, which meant I was on the lookout for my next gig almost before my current one had started.

Denis's next job was *A Funny Thing Happened on the Way to the Forum* at the Williamstown Theatre Festival that summer. It was a show I had done in high school at the Dundee Dinner Theater, and I loved it. At the time I was too young to be playing the role of Hero (especially at seventeen, being cast opposite a woman who was thirty-five), but now, at thirty, I was ready to tackle that show again. Having just been through a casting process with Denis, I knew I could do this on my own. I didn't want to go down that road with him again. The show's plot heavily involves sexy female courtesans and mistaken identities, so the director's decision to make all the characters men seemed like a big swing but also like a fun challenge. Fortunately, the producers and director agreed that I could just come to the callback, which put me on a shorter list.

Unfortunately, the callback was on a matinee day at the

Paper Mill, so this required me to get a car back to the city immediately following our matinee, make my appointment time, nail my audition, and then race back to the theater on New Jersey Transit for the second show. It was hectic, but I felt confident it would be worth it. The day came, I cranked out a matinee for a few hundred sleeping senior citizens, and I raced out of that theater into a waiting taxi. I got to that audition and I was ready to wow them. I truly can't remember if Denis was there. I feel like he wasn't. But maybe I am choosing to forget that he was. In any event, I did all my material and then stood there expecting some adjustment or feedback, and instead the director just said, "Thank you." That was it. "Thank you." I did all the material, exactly once, and then caught the train back to the Paper Mill.

I was pissed. I knew I didn't get it. I knew I didn't even register as a contender for the part. I was angry with the outcome. And I am embarrassed to say I was unjustifiably angry with Denis for not helping me in some way. I was hustling my ass off to stay afloat and make a name for myself in this business. It was hard, and it was humiliating some of the time. I felt like anytime I took one step forward, I fell two steps back. I was tired and looking for assistance, and I mistakenly placed that responsibility on my boyfriend, who I felt had some kind of responsibility to help me.

It wasn't fair to Denis. I put him in an impossible position and I feel bad about it now. I didn't behave well that night at home. I cried, I yelled. He cried, he yelled. We ultimately held each other and I was able to admit that I was scared. I was scared that all my hard work wasn't paying off and that I might burn out before I had really even started. Denis and I recovered pretty quickly in the moment. We still loved each other, we had just seen new sides of each other. But our relationship was never the same.

After all my crying and yelling that night, it would only be a few weeks before I was cast as Elder Price in *The Book of Mormon*. This is why so many actors seem unstable. You can be completely directionless and penniless with no prospects one day, and the next day you are starring in a hit Broadway show. The whiplash can leave you dizzy.

Through the entire workshop process of *The Book of Mormon,* Denis was working out of town. He never got to see the final presentation that ultimately cemented the show's moving to Broadway. And I never saw the show he was doing out of town. When I started rehearsing the show, Denis was again working out of town. At the time it felt like a bit of a gift because I was exhausted when I got home each night and didn't have much to give in terms of affection or conversation. But I missed him. I could have used his support during that time. He probably could have used my support on his show, too. I think we both just lost ourselves in our work.

The first time Denis saw my show was a preview performance a few weeks before we opened. I remember his coming to my dressing room after the show and saying to me, "This is going to be huge for you." But the way he said it was sort of sad. There was something happening between us that I guess I didn't want to admit. We had grown apart because we had been so focused on our work. If I could go back, I would address it right there in my dressing room. I would talk to him and sort out whatever was shifting. But I didn't. Instead I just said, "Thank you."

The show opened and it was a hit. Everything I had hoped would happen did. And two days before the Tonys, Denis broke up with me. He told me that my life was headed in a different direction than his and we should probably call it quits. *What the hell does that mean?* I thought. But I knew what he meant. Years earlier, my first serious boyfriend had broken up with me days after I was cast in my first Broadway show. He was an actor who was also trying to get a break on Broadway. After I told him my good news, he said to me, "You beat me." I didn't think we were competing, but apparently we were. While Denis was not an actor and his choice of phrase was much more civilized, I knew this scene. I had played a version of it before and I still remembered my lines.

I didn't argue with Denis. I didn't scream, I didn't yell. He didn't scream, he didn't yell. My ego got the better of me in that moment. I didn't want to be the one crying and asking for forgiveness or patience. I was sad and hurt, mostly by the situation we had found ourselves in, and particularly by my role in it. While I had been focusing on what happened at that theater, I had let my home life get empty. But I didn't admit to any of that. Instead, I asked him if we could wait until Tuesday to officially break up. I had to perform on the Tony Awards that Sunday, and on Monday morning, I was filming my third episode of *Girls*. My Nebraskan practicality popped up and I decided to schedule my heartbreak for a more convenient time.

Tuesday arrived and we had yet another sad conversation about "not moving in the same direction," I suppose just to clarify any feelings that might have changed in the past few days. It could have been my chance to fight for this relationship, but I didn't fight. I thought for a moment Denis might have changed his mind. He had not, or if he had, he didn't say it. I called my friend Kevin and asked if I could sublet his apartment for a few months. I lugged my life in boxes down five flights of stairs from Denis's apartment, and lugged that life up five flights to Kevin's, and then I tried as best I could to plow ahead. I was in the middle of a huge career change, the most exciting professional time of my life, and I refused to let this breakup overshadow that. So I decided to not feel anything, to numb myself with work. That sufficed for a while, but there were many moments, quiet moments—coming home from work, arriving at a party alone, making dinner for myself with just the TV for company—when I felt very lonely. I missed Denis. I missed the life I'd thought I was creating with him. In the storybook sense, my heart had broken.

It is always so much easier to see the fix to a situation with some distance, with slightly new eyes. Sometimes when I am watching a play or a movie, something that I personally had nothing to do with creating, I will catch myself thinking, *This scene would have worked so much better if they had just changed that one line.* Or, *If that actor had played this scene with more tenderness or just given more of a pause in that moment, the whole story could have landed differently.* It's easy to make those adjustments from the outside. It's harder when you are the character in the middle of it.

Jump ahead six years. I was once again nominated for a Tony. There were the luncheons and press conferences and pictures to take, but this time, guess who was also there? Denis. He was also nominated, for Best Choreography. I saw him at a party for the nominees, from across the Rainbow Room. He looked the same. I wondered if I did.

AND HOW DOES THAT
MAKE YOU FEEL?

———

Trigger warning: i am going to discuss something that I personally find exhausting when other people discuss it. But on the advice of loved ones, I decided to go ahead and share. I will now discuss . . . my relationship with therapy.

I know! I know! No one wants to hear, "Well, my therapist says . . ." But this is a bit of a deeper dive than that. It's about my relationship to therapy and why, at times, it's been as fraught as my dating history, but mostly has really been a lifesaver. If you haven't tried it, I recommend it at least once in your life. Maybe several times, as it often takes a while to find the right therapist. And I'm not saying that the same way people say, "Have you been skydiving? You should!" Or, "Going vegan is life-changing!" Maybe my life is less full for not trying those things, but I just can't right now. Maybe later.

The first time I saw a therapist was sophomore year of college. I had started having panic attacks and did not know what was happening to my body. I finally called my mother to talk about it, and she quickly diagnosed me with anxiety. She had struggled for decades with panic and yet we had never discussed it. I knew she saw a therapist, but I didn't know exactly why, and honestly, I'd never asked. Once we started talking about my struggles, she opened up about hers, and I have to say, I have never felt closer to my mom. She told me about her therapist and her medication, and she really spoke to me like a friend about all this. The first thing she told me was that I should find a professional to talk to. The next thing she did was send me a care package of candy and snacks and a small bottle of her own Xanax. (I am aware that one should not share medication, but she is my mother and she was trying to be helpful.) While I was hesitant to try the pills, I did find myself a therapist with the help of my college counselor. He recommended that I speak to someone at Student Health. I made an appointment and cautiously showed up to have my head shrunk.

The therapist was not much older than I was, and I was unsettled by her quietness. The only thing she kept saying was "And how does that make you feel?" It was infuriating. *I don't know how I feel! That's why I am here! Tell me how I*

feel! It was a bit of a wash of an experience. I never went
back. Instead, I went to Barnes & Noble and found some
books on anxiety attacks. The most helpful one was by a
man named Gary Zukav called *The Seat of the Soul.* It broke
down panic attacks in very broad terms and gave some
helpful suggestions about how to deal with them. For a
couple of years, I felt like Gary and his book were all I
needed. I would refer back to it often, and soon it was just
weathered beyond belief and filled with notes in the mar-
gins. I carried it with me almost everywhere.

Eventually, Gary's words stopped having the same effect on me. I couldn't keep referring to the same old pas-
sages for comfort. I needed to open up to someone again.
This time, it was my friend Jenn. She had always been a
source of comfort and guidance, and I looked to her as a
big sister of sorts while far away from my own family. I
explained my panic predicament. She immediately understood, having struggled with it herself, and quickly recommended that I talk to her therapist, a man named Thomas.

Thomas had a unique technique that echoed Gary Zukav's. It was more active than my college counselor's. He
asked probing questions, he had suggestions, and he recommended exercises for when I was feeling particularly
panicked. I left that first session feeling lighter and calmer
and like I had a set of skills I could actually use. I decided
that I would continue to see Thomas on a regular basis.

As the months passed, I always left my sessions with a

blueprint to help me get through whatever I was struggling with at the moment. At that time, it was mostly career concerns or boyfriend troubles, pretty minor stuff. And then, my dad died. Very suddenly. I wasn't prepared for it—none of us were—and there was a lot of business around dying that I didn't expect. I had to snap into action with my family to plan his funeral, close his business, shut down bank accounts and telephone services. I couldn't allow myself to mourn him in the moment because there was too much to do. Maybe that is overly practical, but that was the route I took. It wasn't until months later, when I was back in New York and had resumed my sessions with Thomas, that I had time to process what had happened. I remember that during my first session back, Thomas sat across from me and asked, "So what's been happening?"

"Well," I started, "my dad died." Then I burst into tears. It was really the first time that I truly cried about it. It felt safe to do in the privacy of this man's office. All of a sudden, after months of appointments with him talking about failed callbacks and bad dates, I had something really big to discuss. I continued to see Thomas on a weekly basis, and he was instrumental in getting me through that time. Again, I felt like I had a map of how to grieve. I don't know how I would have gotten through those first months without him.

Months turned into a year and I continued seeing Thomas. So did a lot of my friends. It was not uncommon to arrive for a session and see someone I had worked with or was working with leave his office in tears. It was always awkward to try to exchange pleasantries with friends who had obviously just been unpacking some emotions moments earlier. It was uncomfortable for all of us.

So many peers were seeing this same man for guidance that it started to feel like a cult. We would compare notes on what Thomas had said to us, talk about which exercises we found helpful. At first, it was nice to have people to talk to about it, but eventually it made me feel weird. This process had started as something private, and now too many of my friends were sharing in the same experience. Then came the day when I was speaking to Thomas about a recent breakup. I could almost see his eyes glazing over from lack of genuine interest, and then he looked at me and said, "Andrew, sometimes what's too painful to remember, we simply choose to forget. So it's the laughter we remember."

I was shocked. "Thomas, did you just quote *The Way We Were* to me?"

He looked stunned and then quickly composed himself. "Ummm . . . yes. Yes, I suppose I did. But it's still good advice."

No. No, it is not good advice. It was Barbra Streisand's advice to millions of people. Why would he think he could get away with that? I'm a gay man! In that moment, I decided that it was time to move on from Thomas.

I didn't see another therapist for many years. In retrospect, it would have been wise to talk to someone while I was going through *The Book of Mormon* and moving to L.A. to start working on television. My life was changing quickly, and while I did a decent job navigating most of it, I had some real messy times along the way. I guess I was nervous about diving into another therapy relationship. My dreams were coming true, right? What did I have to be worried about? But then, while I was doing *Falsettos*, I started having some real relationship issues with my boyfriend at the time, Mike. My friend Rachel recommended we see her couple's therapist, Dan. Mike and I discussed it and we came to the conclusion that it was worth a shot.

Dan was slightly older than us and a gay man, which we saw as a plus. He was patient and kind and not afraid to weigh in on our troubles. He wasn't trying to keep us together, he was trying to help us see the healthiest way forward, whatever that was for us. I think it was our second session when we started to see some red flags. As I was discussing some problems we'd begun to have while living in L.A., Dan asked, "Was this when you were on *The New Normal?*" I had not discussed my profession or my résumé with him.

"Yes, it was around that time."

"I loved that show, by the way. Please, continue."

But I didn't want to continue. I felt like something had cracked. In our next session he told us that he had just seen *Falsettos* and loved it. Again, it felt weird for him to be talking about that with me. Maybe that's not fair to him—he is just a human, after all—but I felt the boundaries were too fuzzy now. At our next session, we really hit a wall. Mike was talking about feeling unseen when he was with me in public. "People look right through me to get to Andrew. It's like I'm invisible. Andrew sucks the air out of every room we walk into, and I feel like I don't even matter."

Dan looked at me and said, "Andrew, did you hear what David just said?"

"Mike."

"I'm sorry?" he replied.

"His name is Mike. Not David."

There was no coming back from that one. It would be the last time we would see Dan. Mike and I still laugh about that moment now, years after breaking up. In some ways it made us closer, though it did not make separating any easier.

Cut to the present, and I once again find myself in therapy. The pandemic sparked all sorts of fear in me and I was feeling wildly untethered. After months of trying to handle it myself, I admitted that I was not equipped to be my own therapist and I sought out a new doctor. This doctor has a more traditional approach and makes you dive into your past to see how it affects your present. It's effective but exhausting. Opening up emotional boxes from your past is interesting but really painful. It has made some things clearer in the present, but it does leave me feeling pretty shitty about my past. This time, to get ahead of my minor celebrity, I just told him, "Doctor, a couple years ago I wrote a book about my early life. Would you mind just reading that so we can skip ahead?" I wasn't sure how he would respond to that, but he agreed and read my first book. I have to say, it was really helpful in our sessions. It brought him up to speed as to how I got where I am today.

It's been over a year since I started seeing him. He's very helpful and very patient, and I have learned a lot about myself through these appointments. But I find myself now needing to take a little break. I'm starting to flatline in our sessions, repeat myself, forgetting what I have already told him. It's not his fault; there's just so much talking I can do about myself. And as an actor, that is really saying something.

I think what I am finding—and I'm sure some in the psychological profession would disagree with me—is that it's more helpful to have a solid therapist on standby. Someone you can check in with periodically to process what's happening around you. Obviously, if you have a major issue or a trauma that you are going through, like I did during the pandemic, regular sessions are key to a healthier life. But for me, right now, I feel like my new doctor and I are going to casually see each other for a bit. It makes our sessions that much more helpful. So far he has never forgotten my name, nor has he ever quoted Barbra Streisand to me.

I think that's a pretty successful relationship, don't you?

IT'S AN HONOR
TO BE ELIGIBLE

———

'VE ALWAYS HAD A COMPLICATED RELATIONSHIP WITH
awards and formal recognition. By that I mean that I
want awards and formal recognition, but sometimes they
don't want me back.

My emotionally abusive relationship with awards started
in junior high. I was doing a lot of community theater and
getting more confident. I had started to find my people, my
"thing" that I was good at, and it gave me ambition, a reason
to dream about my future.

My roles had introduced me to a small organization in
Omaha called the Theater Arts Guild, or TAG, not to be
confused with SAG, the Screen Actors Guild. TAG is like
SAG in that it involves actors, but there are no screens and
much less plastic surgery. Every year they had awards for
the best of the best in Omaha theater. Once I really started

to focus on theater, I had those TAG Awards on lockdown. I have three and I am very proud of all of them.

I only lost once, and now I can't remember who beat me. I know I was nominated for my very broad portrayal of Baby John in *West Side Story*. I think the other kid was maybe Oliver in *Oliver!* It was a much larger role than mine, I remember that. Anyway, he deserved it. I just made the bold choice as Baby John to cry a lot. Like in almost every scene, I found a reason for him to cry. I don't think there was a director for that show. . . . But I digress.

After my early success at the TAGs, I had to wait fourteen years for my next acting award nomination, but this time it was at a slightly larger production than the TAG Awards: the Tony Awards. Spoiler: I haven't won a Tony. This essay does not end with me clutching one and weeping live on CBS. But here are my favorite milestones in brushing shoulders with that little trophy over the years.

2005: AS AN ATTENDEE
(but I Paid for My Ticket)

THE FIRST TIME I attended the Tonys, I was just an audience member—in more ways than one. It was my first year in *Hairspray,* and two of my castmates—Bryan and my good friend Julie Halston—and I decided to get tickets together. We didn't really have a reason to go, but it seemed like an exciting evening and I was a part of the Broadway community now, right? I could be a part of the celebration in person!

As I recall, we got there pretty early. We had a matinee that day, got dressed up after, and still had some time to kill. And there are few people I'd rather kill time with than Julie Halston. Yes, she is a successful actor—a real New York legend—but more than that, she is a personality. A big, big personality. She took me under her wing at *Hairspray* and was my Broadway fairy godmother, and I will always be grateful to her for that. When we arrived at Radio City Music Hall, a buzzy mix of people was milling about on the red carpet—celebrities, famous Broadway producers, nominees. It was very exciting to see up close. We quietly collected our tickets, and Bryan and I looked to Julie for guidance as to what to do next.

"Let's get a drink!" she said. "There are always Tony parties nearby. We can just pop in and grab some champagne."

It sounded very glamorous to go to a Tony party, even if we weren't invited. Julie walked with extreme confidence to the bar at Rockefeller Center, the one that they set up on the ice rink in the spring and summer. It was clearly closed for a private event. I started to get nervous. "Don't we need tickets or something?" I asked in a very midwestern way.

"No! We look great, and we are all on Broadway. We just walk in and act like we belong because we do!"

We followed Julie's lead. No one was asking for tickets,

so maybe she was right? A waiter immediately offered us champagne and within seconds we were standing in the middle of a black-tie party. A few people came over to tell Julie that they had loved seeing her in one production or another, but for the most part, people didn't seem to notice us.

"Who are all these people, Julie?" I asked. "I don't recognize any of them."

"Oh, they are probably all money people. Producers. All the stars are on the red carpet getting their pictures taken."

As we grabbed another champagne, an older man in a tuxedo came over to us. He was wearing a boutonniere, which I thought was odd.

"So what brings you three out tonight?" he asked suspiciously through a tense smile.

Bryan and I froze. Julie took the wheel.

"Just celebrating! It's such an exciting evening."

"Yes, it really is," the smiling old man said. "And you are all friends with . . ."

But before he could finish that sentence, a voice came over the speaker system: "Ladies and gentlemen, please help us welcome the bride and groom, Mr. and Mrs. Giordano!"

A young woman in a very large wedding dress suddenly appeared. She was wearing a huge ornate veil and sobbing tears of, hopefully, joy. She was followed by a man in a tux, smoking a cigar, looking real smug.

Oh fuck. This isn't a Tony party. It's a Sopranos *wedding.*

We all froze but then politely applauded the happy couple. Without conferring with us, Julie looked at the older man and said, "She's a lovely bride! Congratulations!" And then the three of us calmly but swiftly walked out of that party.

Once a safe distance away, we all burst into laughter. "Who has a fucking wedding on the day of the Tonys in Rockefeller Center?!" Julie shouted. "Sorry, boys, but at least we got our champagne! Let's get inside!"

Our seats were in the back of the first balcony of Radio City. If you have never been inside Radio City, it is a cathedral. It's shocking how big it is. The first balcony feels like it's a football field away from the stage. But I was still in the room and thrilled and excited to be there. The last time I had been in Radio City was when I was performing in *Pokémon Live!* It was a fever dream of a show that involved puppets, bad pop ballads, and me in a purple wig. Needless to say, this was a much better reason to be there.

As we watched the show, even from that distance, I was in awe of where I was. After years of watching the Tonys on TV, here I was in the theater, watching them unfold live, and I couldn't believe it. But there was a small voice inside me that kept whispering. . . .

Next time you come to these awards, you are going to be on that stage.

I didn't know how, but I wanted to try.

2009: ON THE STAGE!
(but Not as a Nominee)

A FEW YEARS LATER, I was back on Broadway, this time as Bob Gaudio in *Jersey Boys*. I loved playing that part, and I was grateful to be given that chance, and with an amazing cast. Jarrod Spector was Frankie, Matt Bogart was Nick, and my old pal from *Pokémon Live!* Dominic Nolfi was Tommy. (All roads seem to lead back to *Pokémon Live!* . . .) Even though *Jersey Boys* had been running for several years at this point, it was still wildly successful and sold out every night. That year marked the show's fifth anniversary on Broadway, and the producers of the Tonys had asked the cast to perform the closing number, "December 1963 (Oh, What a Night)," as the finale of the telecast. I was going to be on that stage! I was going to be singing and dancing at the Tonys!

We had a matinee that day and then a long break before we had to be at the theater. An odd detail about performing on the Tonys: Because backstage space is limited, the shows get ready at their own theaters. Then a bus picks you up and takes you to Radio City, where you sit in the bus until it's time for you to perform. It's not as glamorous as I maybe imagined it would be, crammed in a bus with your cast on the street, but it did not dampen the excitement of performing on that stage on Broadway's biggest night.

During our break in between shows, Matt Bogart asked

me to go look at an apartment that he and his wife were thinking about buying. It seemed like an odd chore on Tony day, but I'd had a crush on Matt since I saw him in *Miss Saigon* in 1997, and at that point I would have gone to a dog fight if he had invited me. So we went to see the apartment. The Realtor mistook us for a gay couple and Matt was happy to play along, calling me "babe" for our tour. "Babe, did you see this closet?" "Babe, there's a washer and dryer in here!" Even though it was pretend, I basked in the attention from Matt. (Google him. You'll understand why.)

The time came to perform, and we were taken off our bus and whisked backstage at Radio City. We were standing in the wings as Alice Ripley accepted her Tony for *Next to Normal*. I could see her hold that trophy and give her speech. I was maybe fifteen feet away from her. And while it wasn't my award, it was the closest I had ever been to seeing one. It looked like it did on TV, only up close it was even more emotional.

What must that feel like? What is she thinking right now? What would I be thinking right now? How do I get to where she is standing?

The performance was a success. The audience loved it, and we all had fun, but what sticks with me is being surprised by how huge the stage is at Radio City. You can't really see any of the balconies from the stage, but you can feel the people out there. It's an odd sensation. You can hear the applause, but you can't quite trust where it is coming from. We had a party afterward and I truly felt like I was a part of the evening and, more important, the Broadway community.

Matt and his wife bought that apartment, by the way. I wonder what the Realtor thought when I was replaced with a wife and a baby.

2011: AS A FIRST-TIME NOMINEE
(and Very Overwhelmed)

IN THE SUMMER OF 2010, just two years after *Jersey Boys*, I was rehearsing the workshop of *The Book of Mormon*. In the blur that followed our March opening, it was suddenly May and the Tony nominations were about to be announced. Not only was the show nominated for Best Musical, which meant we would be performing on the Tonys, I was nominated for best actor in a musical.

Best. Actor.

People had told me that my nomination was a sure thing, but in the moment of listening to the announcements, fear had crept in. What if it didn't happen? Lots of people get snubbed every year. But it had happened. The show received fourteen nominations total, the most of any show that year. It was astounding to be met with such appreciation for doing something that I loved so much.

The thing I quickly learned about the Tony Awards process is that it is a full schedule of press and luncheons, and all the while, you have to keep doing your show at night. It's like adding a part-time job on top of a full-time job of eight shows a week. I was running on adrenaline for the following month. Anytime I felt too tired to go on, I just reminded myself that this was exactly what I had always dreamed of. This was the goal. That thought always gave me the burst of energy I needed to get out on that stage. It was also helpful that my co-stars Josh Gad, Nikki James, and Rory O'Malley were nominated as well. We all got to go through that head-spinning process together. If we weren't already family, that month really solidified it.

About a week after the nominations came out, I got a call from our lead producer, Scott Rudin. Scott rarely called, and when he did, it was often tense. You had done something wrong; you had upset him in some way. A lot has come out about Scott and the way he treated his assistants. Horrible stories. I was never his assistant, but as one of the leads in a very successful show he was producing, I know how he spoke to me, so I can only imagine what they all went through. He was a scary man. Powerful, intimidating. I tried my best to stay out of his eye line and just do my job as best I could.

Seeing his name pop up on my phone that day filled me with dread. Was I being fired? Did I offend him? It was neither of those things. Instead, he told me that he and the creative team had been talking and they'd decided that the best number to perform at the Tonys that year was "I Believe," my character's eleven o'clock number. (That's showbiz talk for a big, belty number right before the end of the show.) "I Believe" was my solo. There were three other actors onstage—Brian Tyree Henry, Tommar Wilson, and John Eric Parker—but in non-singing roles. Scott was asking me to sing my solo number at the Tony Awards. All I could think was, *Is this possible? Is this really going to happen? Is this a prank?*

Word quickly spread through the cast that "I Believe" would be our Tony number. While I was thrilled, I was also conflicted. Usually the Tony number for a nominated show features the whole company. Sometimes it's a medley to show off as many numbers as possible. Ours would be just one—mine. I was worried that the rest of the cast would be angry, especially Josh, Nikki, and Rory, who were also nominated. I remember talking to them each about this and they were all very supportive. If they were disappointed, they hid it well. I couldn't have asked for better friends in that moment.

The day finally came, that first Sunday in June when the Tonys are usually held, and I felt ready. I felt focused. I felt . . . alone. As you now know, my boyfriend Denis had broken up with me two days earlier. I was heartbroken but decided to focus on the job at hand. I would feel all that later, I told myself. Sunday afternoon, I put on my tuxedo; I got in a car with Denis, who was still going to be my date that night (I should have thought that through better, but I was in the emotional weeds, folks. I couldn't deal with a last-minute date change!); and I headed to the Tonys.

As a nominee, if you are performing, you get pulled from your seat about an hour before your performance so that you can change, get makeup, and get mic'd up. It all started to feel real. Like for-real real. I was going to have to sing this song. My nerves kicked in. I started feeling unsteady. Could I still run? Should I get in a cab and disappear? As the sound technician was snaking a wire all over my body, a man tapped me on the shoulder. I turned and had to look up to see his face, and at six feet two that's not something I often have to do. Standing in front of me, looking like a black-tie god, was Hugh Jackman. He literally took my breath away.

"I saw your show and I just wanted to say how much I enjoyed your performance," he said in his charming Australian accent. "Just incredible." (I'm really a sucker for those Aussies.)

"Oh, thank you! That means so much to me. I am a huge fan."

He smiled. "I hear you are performing your big number tonight. That's exciting."

My big number. Yes, I was about to perform my big number at the Tony Awards in front of a live audience of six thousand people and millions more in homes across the country. I would be alone onstage representing a show that had changed my entire life. This all hit me at once with breakneck speed. I was at the Tonys talking to Hugh Jackman as a nominee for best actor in a musical. My legs felt weak. What the fuck was I doing here? I didn't belong here. This was all too much.

"How are you feeling?" Hugh asked with a smile.

"Honestly, I am very nervous." I wasn't about to lie to Hugh Jackman.

"Come here," he said. He hugged me and squeezed tightly and kind of rocked me back and forth very subtly. "You are going to be great," he said.

I did not know Hugh Jackman, nor had I ever met him, but I squeezed him back and breathed deeply for a second. Then he gave me a hard pat on the back and released me.

"Thank you," I said.

He smiled. "Go get 'em."

Oh, Hugh Jackman. He'll never know how much I needed that moment. I was overwhelmed and feeling very alone, and the fact that he took a second to reassure a stranger that everything was going to be okay still means so much to me.

I made my way backstage and took my place behind a wall of monitors at the spot where I would make my entrance. It was very hot from all the screens and wires on the wall.

"You'll be up right after this award," a stage manager told me.

The other *Book of Mormon* actors who would join me onstage were entering from another part of the stage. I didn't even get to see them before our performance. I was alone. Then I heard, "The nominees for Best Featured Actress in a Musical are . . ."

It was Nikki's category. I didn't know that it was happening right before my performance. As Harry Connick, Jr., read the names of the nominees, any anxiety that Hugh Jackman had put at bay came rushing back. I was as nervous for her as I would have been for myself. And then . . . they called her name. Nikki won! I started to cry backstage as I listened to my friend accept her award. Nikki is a brilliant actor and was astonishing in *The Book of Mormon*. It was a well-deserved win for her.

As the music played her off the stage, I heard Stephen Colbert being introduced. It was about to happen. I had to pull it together. This was the moment I had been imagining since I'd first seen the Tonys on television years before. All my pretending to be Brent Carver in *Kiss of the Spider Woman* during his Tony performance in 1993 had hopefully prepared me for my very own Tony moment. This was it! And then, all the moisture left my mouth. I was completely dry. I looked around for someone to bring me some water, but there was no one. It was too late. Stephen Colbert said my name and the wall of monitors flew up, revealing me. I heard applause and then the orchestra started. I was on.

As I write this, I am sweating at the memory. What I

remember most from the performance is that my lips were sticking to my teeth from a lack of saliva. I was desperately trying to produce spit to help me get through that number. I hit all my marks, I could hear the audience laughing, and I was just praying that I could make it to the end. I was so relieved when Brian Tyree Henry appeared by my side and I could take his hand. I needed a friend. I needed a touchstone from our nightly performances. The number ended, and once again I heard a wall of applause. And just like that, it was over. I made my way backstage to change back into my tuxedo and took my seat next to my now ex-boyfriend. There was a huge energy crash and I just wanted to lie down. But the show wasn't over yet. I still had to get through my category. As I sat there and watched the rest of the show, I kept replaying my performance in my head.

Was I terrible? Was that awful? Could people tell I could barely swallow?

Denis assured me that it was great. Scott Rudin came to my seat to congratulate me, as did my other castmates seated nearby. Patti LuPone gave me a thumbs-up from several rows over. I had to trust it was fine. Patti doesn't lie!

I convinced myself that I would not win my category. Josh and I were both nominated, and I told myself that we would cancel each other out. It didn't matter, I told myself. I was there, I was nominated, and I had just sung alone at the Tony Awards. That all meant a win for me. Then the category came up. I relaxed my face into the gracious-loser pose I knew I would need. A camera operator came rushing up to my seat with a camera dangerously close to my face to catch my reaction. Catherine Zeta-Jones started reading the names. In that moment, in those thirty seconds of reading the nominees, my mind drifted.

I guess I could win. . . . Why not? Why couldn't I win? I want to win!

"And the winner is . . . Norbert Leo Butz!"

It was not me. The moment was over and the camera operator raced away as if he had never been there. I took a deep breath.

Now it's done. Your job is over for the evening.

2017: AS A SECOND-TIME NOMINEE
(and Feeling Much More Relaxed)

IN THE YEARS THAT FOLLOWED, I often returned to the Tonys. I performed a number with Neil Patrick Harris, Laura Benanti, and Megan Hilty. I presented awards with Saoirse Ronan and Sutton Foster. I am honored every time they ask me back.

Then in 2017, I returned to the Tonys, but this time as a nominee again. I had the great honor of playing Whizzer in the revival of *Falsettos*. I was nominated for Best Featured Actor in a Musical, and once again I was surrounded by three fellow cast members who were also nominated: Christian Borle, Stephanie J. Block, and Brandon Uranowitz. This time, since we were also nominated for Best Revival of a Musical, our number would be performed by the entire company. We had closed months earlier, so it was a real thrill to get to reunite our whole cast again.

My *Falsettos* experience was perhaps the best of my professional life. That was the closest I have ever felt to a cast before. There were only seven of us in total, which is pretty rare for a musical. There was a love that grew between us all, partly because of the nature of the story we were telling every night but also because every one of us was honored to be in that cast. *The Book of Mormon* was incredible for many other reasons, but because I was new to the scene, everything sort of flew by in a blur. This time, I was a little older and hopefully a lot wiser, and I took time to take in all the joy that was surrounding me. It was helpful too that *Falsettos* had closed, so instead of rushing to do the show every night, we all just got to enjoy the Tony nomination process. (Meaning I could have a glass of wine at the luncheons and not worry about it.) I had fun, I met people, I forced a friendship with Laura Linney! I loved the whole experience.

About that time, I came across a book that the great Ellen Burstyn wrote several years ago called *Lessons in Becoming Myself*. I can't recommend it enough. I am just in awe of Ellen and her incredible talent, and I admire the honesty with which she wrote about her career. In the book, she talks about being nominated for an Academy

Award for *Requiem for a Dream*. If you haven't seen the film, it's a tough watch because of the dark subject matter, but you will be hard-pressed to find a better performance on-screen than Ellen's. This was also the same year that Julia Roberts was nominated for *Erin Brockovich*. Ellen writes that while she knew *Requiem for a Dream* was the greatest performance of her life, she also knew it was Julia Roberts's moment that year. She was winning all the awards leading up to the Oscars, and it was clear Julia would probably take home that trophy, too. Ellen made her peace with that.

Taking a page from Ellen's book, literally, I also accepted that this was not going to be my Tony. I was and am incredibly proud of my work as Whizzer. I feel it's the best work I have ever done. While I would have happily accepted that Tony, I knew it was not my year. Maybe that's why I had so much fun leading up to the awards that season. Every party, every junket, I was just thrilled to be there again. The night of the awards, with Zuzanna by my side, I had fun. The red carpet before the show felt like a celebration. Our performance was filled with love and an electric happiness. It was a perfect night.

I mean, my calm might have also had something to do with the fact that I herniated a disc in my lower back at a Tonys rehearsal and I was high on painkillers all weekend, but I would like to think that Ellen's words and my gratitude for the experience also had something to do with it.

Since then, I have been back to the Tonys many times. I have a blast every time. It's never not a thrill and a humbling experience to remember little Andy Rannells in Omaha obsessively watching every June as dreams came true on that stage.

While I don't have my own personal Tony, I also understand that trophies of any kind don't really change anything. Awards are fickle. They taunt you with their existence, they promise acceptance and professional fulfillment, but they end up just moving on to someone else before you know it. In the end, the work is still the work, and the desire to keep getting to perform, to keep doing the thing that you love, will always be there regardless of the fullness of your trophy case.

Would it be nice to have a Tony? Absolutely! Would it ultimately make me happier? Probably not. But I guess I'll never know until I have one. . . .

I'm looking at you, Tony voters!

THE WATER BOTTLE TOUR
OF L.A.

———

B Y THE TIME I WAS THIRTY-THREE I HAD DECIDED, based on *Helter Skelter*, multiple rewatchings of *Clueless* and *Sunset Boulevard*, and one three-day trip to Los Angeles, that L.A. was not for me. I didn't like driving, home invasions seemed far too common, and I was confused by the city zoning laws. Why was there a house next to a nail salon next to another house next to an Arby's? Who was planning this place? Besides, I was a theater actor. What need did I have for L.A.?

But after *The Book of Mormon* opened, the West Coast started calling to me. Within a couple of months I had a Hollywood manager and invitations to take meetings with a slew of L.A. creative types and the heads of every major television network. Los Angeles suddenly seemed more appealing.

I took a week off from *The Book of Mormon* and flew out to see what these meetings might have to offer. It was an exciting trip but overwhelming. I love a list of tasks, and this trip had one solid goal: I had to get my own television show. I was told by many people who seemed to know way more than I did that I had to jump on the opportunities that *Mormon* had provided me.

One of the opportunities it had already provided me was a role on HBO's *Girls*. Lena Dunham and Jenni Konner offered me the role of Elijah, Lena's character's ex-college boyfriend. It was supposed to be one episode, but that turned into two and then three, and before I knew it, I was a regular part of that cast. It was a beautiful surprise, and I loved being on that show. I loved that I did *Mormon* by night and played Elijah by day. It was more than I could have dreamed of or asked for.

As we finished the first season of *Girls,* the voices in my ear were now telling me that it was time for me to be the lead of my own show. I talked to Lena about it and she graciously invited me to stay with her while she was in L.A. editing season one of *Girls*. (The show wouldn't premiere on television for a few more months.) "I think you should take some meetings," she told me. But she added, "Just know everyone you meet is going to have a job for you. When you leave every meeting you are going to feel like you left with a movie or a TV show. Everyone is going to say that they want to work with you immediately. And

I'm sure they do, but the real trick is to see who actually calls." She also said, "And everyone is going to offer you a bottle of water. You won't drink it, but just take it. This is the water bottle tour of L.A."

I was excited for my free water and the promise of fame in L.A. My agent at the time, Robert Attermann at Abrams Artists, and my new Hollywood manager, Christie Smith, had set up a head-spinning number of meetings for me that week. In all, I had twenty scheduled over five days. I would be meeting with showrunners, producers, and network executives. I knew some of the names but most were new to me. I started off my week with hope, a rented Chevy Cobalt, and a Garmin I wasn't sure how to work. But I was there, damn it! I was ready to go west and stake my claim in Hollywood!

I'm not going to bore you with every meeting, but I will give you the highlights. My first meeting was with Seth Rogen and Evan Goldberg at Point Grey Pictures. They were funny and charming, they both smelled strongly of weed, and they said that they wanted to find a project to work on with me. While Lena's words were fresh in my mind, there was something about Seth and Evan that I believed—they gave me the impression that they didn't have time for bullshit or hyperbole. I felt like I would work with them. (Spoiler: It took six years, but they indeed found a project to work on with me. It's called *Black Monday*. See! I was right!)

I should also mention that in addition to Lena, there was another New Yorker from my life in L.A. that week: my friend Mike. It was complicated because we also happened to be in the middle of a fraught, sometimes sexual relationship. I would say it was an emotional affair, but oftentimes penises were involved. I had taken a stand with Mike recently and told him our friendship could not continue. I was really having feelings for him and he was still in a relationship—an open relationship, but a relationship nonetheless. I had been down that road before with Denis and I didn't want to do it again. I was going to make better choices, damn it. So while I knew Mike was in town, I wasn't certain that I was going to see him. I bored Lena with all the details of this saga. She very patiently listened and gave solid advice well beyond her twenty-four years of age. That week we were really living *Girls LIVE!* Often she would come home from editing, I would have spent the entire day pimping myself out for future work, and we would open a bottle of Pinot Grigio, order sushi, and watch *The Bachelor* on TV. It was a cozy week and I loved it.

One night, my meetings took me to the east side, which was where Mike was staying. I felt compelled to tell him I was nearby. We made a plan: I would come over, we would order dinner, and then we would watch Ryan Murphy's new show, *American Horror Story.* It would be a very tame, very nonsexual evening. We were just friends, and that sounded like a very "friend" activity to me. I could control myself and not act on my attraction to Mike. We watched *American Horror Story* and I loved it. It was incredible. So scary, so well acted. Ryan Murphy was not on my list of meetings for the week, and I was instantly disheartened about that. We finished the episode and I said good night to Mike, once again vowing to myself that I would not see him in the future because it was simply too emotionally confusing for me.

When I got back to Lena's, I updated her on my resolve to move forward without Mike and my new obsession with *American Horror Story*. We both turned in early because she had a morning of editing and I had a meeting with the then president of CBS, Nina Tassler.

"Look at us!" I said before heading to bed. "We are Hollywood movers and shakers!"

The next morning I began my trek to CBS. I put on my "Hollywood meeting outfit," which consisted of jeans, Red Wing boots, some version of a plaid shirt from J.Crew, and the appropriate blazer, either navy or gray. (I was going for a "sexy substitute teacher" vibe. A teacher whom you could call by his first name and who would curse in class. *A cool guy.*) I got in my Cobalt. "Garmin," I said, "don't fail me now! I'm coming for you, Nina Tassler!"

My Garmin slightly betrayed me, however, or maybe I just was paying too much attention to my pre-meeting prep. *Hello, Ms. Tassler! Why yes, I do see myself as a perfect combination of Scott Bakula and Allison Janney! Thank you for agreeing with me!* All of a sudden, I had to make a left turn and I was firmly in the far-right lane. Panic and poor driving skills set in and I missed my turn. I got stressed out by Garmin's frantic attempts to reroute me and I decided the best thing was to pull over to redirect myself. I enthusiastically made a sharp right turn into a gas station, missing the driveway, jumping a curb, and popping a tire.

I knew what I had done immediately but I was in denial. *Who needs tires?! I have ambition!* I thought. *I will drive this Cobalt on its rims to CBS, have my meeting, and then deal with the fact that I destroyed a rental car.* And then the car started to make very odd noises and a man in a car next to me shouted, "You have a flat tire, asshole!" Reality set in. I still had forty-five minutes before my meeting and I was only a couple of blocks away. I could park the car, call the rental company, and then reassess after my meeting. I looked at my schedule. To my horror, I only had about thirty minutes between this meeting and my next meeting, with Disney executives on the Disney lot. I had always seen myself as a Prince Eric from *The Little Mermaid,* so this was tricky. I weighed my options: 1) I could try to reschedule Disney and then deal with the car. 2) I could hitchhike to Disney Studios. Or 3) I could call someone for help.

Readers, keep in mind that this was pre-Uber. If this were happening today, I probably wouldn't be driving at all, but here I was in the middle of L.A., not knowing where in the hell I was and freaking the fuck out about the timing of these meetings. I caved. I called Mike and explained the situation. I said, "I could just reschedule Disney." Mike was adamant: "You are here to take these meetings, so take them. Leave the car parked at the gas station, walk the two blocks to your meeting, and I'll pick you up at CBS and drive you to Disney. You can deal with the car after that. Focus on what you came here to do."

You know how sometimes you just want to be taken care of? You just want to be saved? I was overwhelmed—by Los Angeles, by these meetings, by my feelings for Mike. I don't really like being taken care of. I like to do things my-self, to be in charge of my adventures. It's not that it makes me feel weak to accept help, it just makes me feel irrespon-sible. I know that's silly, but my pioneer ancestors instilled in me the feeling of "I can do it myself, damn it!" But this time I leaned into being a damsel in distress. I let Mike pick me up and drive me to my meetings. It was the right choice. I needed help, I needed to be saved. Did I need to be saved by someone else's boyfriend? Probably not. But asking for help was the first step.

I nailed my meetings and everyone promised me jobs. I called the rental car company, got a new car, and then made it back to Lena's in time to order burritos and decompress. I told her about the day and we laughed about how right she was about all these meetings. Everyone was telling me that they had shows ready for me to star in immediately. I was grateful to her for giving me the heads-up about Hollywood lingo like "So you're tech avail after March?" and "You have pilot outs, yeah?" I also told her about Mike and the rescue and how I felt happy and weak all at the same time. She listened and then she said, "It seems like he just gave you a ride. You still had to do all the hard stuff." I thought about it. *Is that true? I guess it is.* I guess I didn't need to be *saved*, I just needed some support.

The week had been overwhelming, and I was putting myself out there in a way that I had never done before, at least not so directly. And even though I knew the deal with these meetings—that I was being promised everything by these people I had never met before and I knew most of these "offers" were not real—it was still messing with my head. This world played by a whole new set of rules and offered new ideas and dreams that I hadn't even known were possible. Did I want these things? Could I even have these things? Would I ever feel successful without these things? It felt like I had just moved my own professional finish line and was at the back of the race.

All of a sudden I wanted to go home. I wanted to go back to *The Book of Mormon* and do what I knew I did well. I already had the job of my dreams. Couldn't I just enjoy that? I didn't need to chase another dream just yet. And as far as Mike went, it was okay to want someone in my life who would share these experiences with me and give me support when I needed it, but I had to look for that in someone who was actually available. I had one day of meetings left. I could handle one more day and then I would go back to my Mormon missionary world, where I could sing and dance like I had always wanted.

I started my last day in L.A. a little numb and a little checked out but grateful for the experience. I was getting used to driving all over L.A. having these meetings, shaking hands, telling stories, taking the free bottles of water. I was still completely reliant on my Garmin, but I knew how to get myself home now. That was the most important thing.

I can't quite recall who I met with that last day, but at lunchtime, I got a phone call from my manager, Christie. "We have one more meeting for you today. How quickly do you think you can get to the Paramount lot? Ryan Murphy wants to meet with you." I'm sorry, what now? Ryan Murphy? *Popular. Nip/Tuck. Glee. American Horror Story.* That Ryan Murphy wants me to come to his office on the Paramount lot? I didn't realize how much I wanted this meeting until I got the call. *This is why I came to L.A.* I was planning on stopping for lunch before I had to head to the airport, but now food seemed unimportant.

As fate would have it, the day before I'd had a meeting at NBC with its then president, Jennifer Salke, and then chairman, Bob Greenblatt. They were very nice and very present during my meeting—two things not everyone was—and they mentioned a project they were developing with Ryan. They didn't give me a ton of details, but they mentioned that it was about a gay couple starting a family with a surrogate. "If you ever meet Ryan, you should ask him about it," Jennifer told me. It had seemed like a long shot because I didn't have a meeting with Ryan, but now I was speeding toward Paramount to sit across from him. This was my moment. What exactly was I asking about or for? No clue. But I knew I had to ask.

The Paramount lot was by far the most "Hollywood" lot I had visited. The whole thing looked like a movie to me. I could easily imagine Betty Grable and Frank Sinatra walking about in beautiful costumes, smoking filterless cigarettes, and shouting at other actors, "Call my girl and we'll set up a dinner at the Brown Derby!" I managed to get there early, so I walked around reading the various plaques on the soundstages: "Mary Pickford worked here." "This is where *Jaws* was filmed." "This way to the Coffee Bean." I wished my dad were with me. He would have loved this.

Ryan's office was located in a building on the Paramount lot called "the Loft." It was ... well, a loft. I walked into Ryan's office space, which looked beautiful and even *smelled* beautiful. It was a perfectly curated space with incredible artwork, big, expensive-looking leather couches, and scented candles placed throughout. Yes, it was an office, but it was also my dream living room. I was intimidated but oddly at ease. Ryan's assistant, Sara, walked me into his office, and there he was, Ryan Murphy. The chat was casual, friendly, and familiar, and I found that we had more in common than I'd thought. We were both from the

Midwest, both raised Catholic, both Old Hollywood ob-
sessed. I felt comfortable with Ryan. He was easy to talk to,
and I felt like we clicked.

"I'm thinking about a role for you on *Glee,* Andrew. It
would be a fun arc." This seemed like a real job. Even sitting
with Ryan for the short time I had, I could tell he didn't fuck
around. If he was saying that there was a job, that there was
an "arc," then there was. *Glee* was incredibly popular at this
time. They were in their second season and everyone was
watching it. A spot on the show would be an incredible opportunity for me. But I remembered Jennifer Salke's words
and I felt compelled—I felt propelled—to ask, "Working on
Glee would be amazing, but . . . I heard you are developing a
show at NBC about a gay couple starting a family. It sounds
really great. Can you tell me more about that?"

Ryan got a very cool look on his face, like shades had
been drawn over his eyes. He didn't look upset, but he
looked intrigued. Or annoyed? I couldn't tell if I had gone
too far. He explained the premise in very broad strokes.
Not a ton of detail, but enough to get the gist. Even with
the little information I had, I knew that I was interested in
this show, in this story.

Girls had taught me that I loved working on television
and telling new, unique stories. I admired Lena so much
for telling her story with such boldness and honesty. I
wanted to do the same thing, but I wanted to tell my story.
The idea of being the lead of a show that centered on a gay

couple starting a family seemed very topical and very fresh. Yes, *Modern Family* existed and what they were doing was groundbreaking, but Ryan's show would be *about* the gay couple. They would be the leads, the center and heart of the show. I knew I had to do it. So that's what I said: "I want to do that show for you, Ryan."

He didn't even blink. "Why do you think that's your show?"

"Because as a gay actor, I want to tell gay stories, stories that we know to be true but that haven't been told yet for a wide audience," I said. "I know you will tell this story with integrity and honesty and I would, too. I think you can only trust a gay actor to tell this story, and I am that actor."

I shocked myself with my own boldness. But I just felt like . . . *Fuck it. How many times am I going to be sitting across from Ryan Murphy?* I had been pitched every version of the gay best friend all week. I didn't want that to be my future, and here was a man who was about to tell a story that interested me. One that I could have some valuable input in telling. I was going to be brave and I was going to ask for what I wanted. So I did. I finished my "I'm just an actor standing in front of a producer asking him to love me" speech and waited for his response. Ryan stared at me for a few seconds. "Okay, that's good to know," he said. "It was great meeting you, Andrew. Travel safely today."

And that was it. Within seconds I was in the parking lot walking toward my Chevy Cobalt and my Garmin. I had blown it. He had offered me a solid job on one of the most popular shows on television and I had blown it. I had overstepped. I called Christie and told her what I had done. Keep in mind that my relationship with her was new. She was taking a chance on me and I might have botched a huge meeting with a huge creator. She listened to the story and said, "It's okay. I'm sure it's not as bad as you think, and you met with a lot of people this week. It's been a great week. Remember that." She was right. It had been a great week and I had made some great connections. Sure, I might have struck out at the one meeting I'd wanted more than anything, but who knew? Maybe Christie was right. Maybe it wasn't that bad.

A month went by. I was back in New York, back in *Mormon* and Uganda. I loved being in that show, telling that story, wearing that short-sleeved shirt. It was *my* role and I had never been prouder to be a part of a show before. To Lena's point, none of those "offers" I was given in my meetings came to fruition. There were no calls, no followups. Everyone had loved meeting me, but that was all that was said. It didn't matter. I was home and I was happy.

A few months later, I found myself without a matinee due to a temporary change in our schedule, and I decided that I wanted to treat myself to a show. It was an easy choice. Bernadette Peters was starring in *Follies* and I wanted more than anything to see one of my heroes live onstage. And in a Sondheim, no less! I went alone to the show, purchasing a fourth-row orchestra seat. I wanted to see Bernadette up close. I was milling around in the lobby before the show, being occasionally recognized by other audience members for my work in *Mormon*. It felt good; it felt great, actually. Here I was about to see one of my idols and I was also the thing I had always dreamed I would be: a Broadway actor. I felt sturdy. Strong. I felt like I had my feet underneath me and my dreams in my hands. It was perhaps the best I had ever felt.

My phone vibrated. It was Christie. I still had about ten minutes before the show, so I answered. "Rannells. Where are you?"

"I'm about to see Bernadette Peters in *Follies*."

"Well that's fun! Honey, I have some news. Are you ready for this? I just got off the phone with Ryan Murphy's office and you got an offer to star in his new pilot for NBC. It's called *The New Normal* and you would be the lead."

I felt certain I didn't understand what she was saying.

"It's an audition?" I asked.

"No, Andrew. It's an *offer*. The show is yours if you want it."

"I want it," I said without hesitating.

"Okay. I will get into the details. See? I told you that the meeting wasn't as bad as you thought."

I hung up, shocked. How had this happened? I mean, I knew how it had happened, but I still couldn't believe it had happened. I sat through *Follies* in a bit of a daze. I would occasionally forget the phone call, usually when Bernadette was onstage, and then I would remember: *You are going to be in a pilot for Ryan Murphy's new show. You are the star of an NBC pilot for Ryan fucking Murphy.* The combination of Bernadette's perfect and heartbreaking performance as Sally and this news made me very emotional. I ended up crying through most of the show. Crying because I was moved; because there was Bernadette Peters; because I had gotten something I wanted. But I think mostly because I might have been leaving Broadway sooner than expected.

Being on Broadway had been my *only* dream. Truly. I wanted to be a Broadway star. I wanted to be Patrick Wilson, Brian d'Arcy James, Brian Stokes Mitchell, Bernadette Peters! I wanted to be them all. Of course I had thought about working on television, but that had seemed very far away, very theoretical. Sure, I had seen people do it. I had watched Kristin Chenoweth's rise to fame with sniperlike focus. I saw that after *You're a Good Man, Charlie Brown,* she got a development deal at NBC, starred in her own series, and then went on to more success on Broadway and on film. I knew that I wanted to follow in her tiny footsteps and that I would try my best to repeat that blueprint. I had been in New York for fourteen years and had gotten used to things taking a while. This all seemed to be happening too quickly.

But the opportunity was here, the door had opened, I had to walk through. *I guess Los Angeles is a place for me after all,* I thought. *Now, how do I become a better driver? . . .*

ALWAYS SIT NEXT
TO MARK RUFFALO

———

I'T'S NOT UNUSUAL FOR ME TO BE SHOUTED AT ON THE streets of New York. It's usually a young woman who has had a few too many mimosas at brunch. She'll scream, "Elijah!" at me like I'm a long-lost grade school friend. I will smile politely and wave, and then she and her friends will all laugh and wave back. That's generally the extent of these interactions.

I guess that's a small price to pay for six exciting and career-altering years playing Elijah Krantz on the HBO show *Girls*. It was a wild time filled with parties and award shows and photo shoots and talk shows and, of course, actually doing the work that made all those fun times possible. Elijah was a character created by Lena Dunham and Jenni Konner, who handed me his shape and then trusted me to fill him up with all the personality and vulnerability and eccentricities and love I could create. Elijah will always be a part of me, as will my six-year *Girls* experience.

If there is one moment that best encapsulates my time in Elijah's knockoff Gucci loafers, it would be the 2015 Golden Globes. The show was nominated for Best Series—Musical or Comedy, and Lena for Best Actress in a Television Series—Musical or Comedy. Lena had graciously invited me to be her date for the evening. I had never been to an awards show like the Golden Globes before.

Yes, I had been to the Tonys many times, but they felt different. They were familiar and cozy, a group of peers all celebrating one another. I imagined the Golden Globes would be more intimidating. I only knew the attendees from seeing them on television and in movies, which made me nervous. All the stars would be there!

I should note that this was before the Hollywood Foreign Press Association (HFPA) was restructured after the public realized that the HFPA lacked racial diversity and some of their members were—what's the best way to say this?—fucking nuts. I can only speak of my personal experience, but anytime I have had interactions with them, mostly through press conferences around the premiere of a show, I have found them to be wildly disorganized and aggressively inappropriate. Maybe they are different now. I certainly hope so.

Because I was new to Hollywood, being Lena's date

seemed like a fun adventure. We had become close over the years, and while we didn't see each other that much when we weren't working together, we would be tight while filming each season. She is such a generous person, and I marveled at her ability to write, direct, and act in that show with such confidence and ease.

For the Golden Globes, I kind of felt like I was going to the prom with Lena. A prom where Meryl Streep would also be in attendance. That night, I met Lena at the Sunset Tower Hotel in Los Angeles. Ralph Lauren had lent me a tuxedo and I was feeling very Old Hollywood. Lena looked stunning in a bright red satin dress, and she had her hair styled in a chic bob like a flapper. I think we nailed our looks.

We were giddy in the car. Lena's stylist didn't want her dress to wrinkle before we arrived at the red carpet, so she was lying down in the backseat. Being a gentleman, I didn't want her to feel awkward, so I lay down next to her. We just laughed at the ridiculousness of it. We got to the red carpet and it was the longest, biggest press line I had ever seen. I was instantly nervous, but I relaxed as soon as I realized that no one really cared that I was there. Everyone was screaming for Lena and I was there to hold her purse and be supportive. I was thrilled I could fill that role for her that evening. We posed for our photos, or mostly Lena posed for her photos, and I stood by and watched and cheered and made sure there wasn't lipstick on her teeth. Lena was very sweet, though, and pulled me into several photos.

We have some fun ones from that night, especially of me and my old pal Matt Bomer. Matt and I met shortly after he graduated from college and moved to New York. He was then and still is one of the most handsome men I have ever encountered. Once the shock of his beauty wears off, you learn he is also one of the kindest people you'll ever encounter. When I saw him on the red carpet, it made me even more relaxed. I was so happy to see a friend there. I photobombed him a couple of times. He was a good sport about it.

The other person who put me at ease on the red carpet was someone I didn't actually know but whom I felt like I had known for a long time: Mario Lopez. He was interviewing people for *Access Hollywood* and trying to get people to do shots of tequila with him. Lena isn't much of a drinker but she warily agreed, while I, on the other hand, jumped at the chance to do a shot with A. C. Slater. (PS: He was as hot in person as I'd hoped he'd be.)

Eventually, I realized that everyone is sort of nervous at events like the Golden Globes. No one feels at home, so you end up having these strange interactions with people that feel very intimate even though you don't know them. Helen Mirren asked me if her forehead was shiny before she started an interview. Bryan Cranston straightened my bow tie as I was about to take a photo. People were looking out for one another, even if they didn't know one another. Just like at the Tonys, there was a common bond of actor insecurity and excitement that brought everyone a little closer for the evening, if only for a moment.

Once we headed inside to make our way to the ballroom, things got even wackier. HBO had a table for Lena, Jemima Kirke, Zosia Mamet, and Allison Williams; a few producers from the show; and the then president of the network, Richard Plepler. It also included one seat for me as Lena's date. At the last minute, Richard Plepler announced that he would also be bringing his wife to the awards, which meant there was one person too many at the table. Guess who got bounced? Spoiler: It wasn't Richard Plepler's wife! It was yours truly. "But don't worry," the HBO publicist told me. "We have a seat for you at the *Foxcatcher* table!"

Foxcatcher is a fantastic film starring Steve Carell, Channing Tatum, and the always dreamy Mark Ruffalo. It's based on a true story about a millionaire eccentric and sociopath who wants to sponsor an Olympic wrestling team. It doesn't go well and it ends in murder. *Foxcatcher* was nominated for Best Drama that year, and Mark Ruffalo and Steve Carell were nominated for acting awards. I really loved that movie and the documentary it is based on, but guess what? I wasn't in that movie, and I didn't know those people!

I'd just started to calm down from the red carpet, and now I had to sit with famous strangers at a table celebrating a film I had nothing to do with. I said hello to my *Girls* friends and then made my way to the *Foxcatcher*s. I know I should have been more excited, but I was nervous and, frankly, embarrassed that I had been bounced from my own show's table. But the social anxiety gods decided to smile upon me that night and gave me a magical gift. When I got to the table and began to awkwardly introduce myself to my famous-stranger tablemates and try to explain why I was there, Mark Ruffalo and his kind wife, Sunrise, enthusiastically stood up to welcome me and told the table how great I was in *The Book of Mormon* and *Girls*. Mark hugged me and pulled my chair out for me, and luckily I was sitting right next to him. I felt immediately more at ease, and no one at the table made me feel weird about being the only non-*Foxcatcher* there.

No one except . . . Sienna Miller. Sienna was seated on the other side of me. I'd always thought she was a great actor and was excited to be next to her. Foolishly, I thought that Mark's glowing introduction might win me some goodwill from her, but when I sat down and attempted to personally introduce myself, she slowly stared at me and looked me up and down with pursed lips, squinting at me like she was trying to make sense of how I had invaded her general vicinity. She curtly said, "Hello," and then proceeded to whisper something to the person next to her, a very attractive woman I would quickly learn was Sienna Miller's publicist and friend. Sienna Miller and her publicist/friend then quickly changed seats so that the publicist was sitting next to me. Sienna Miller was now safely one seat away from the odd television interloper. The publicist/friend introduced herself and seemed very nice, and I felt bad for her that she had to sit next to me. But the awards telecast was about to begin, so there probably wouldn't be time for too much chitchat anyway.

Tina Fey and Amy Poehler were hosting that year, and I have to say, their opening monologue was one of the funniest things I have ever seen live. I love both of those women to an obsessive degree, so to see them in person was a lifetime highlight. They had a run of jokes about *Foxcatcher* and the cameras kept throwing to the table—our table. I couldn't help but wonder if people at home, and perhaps some people in the room who hadn't seen the film, were thinking, *Was Elijah from* Girls *in* Foxcatcher?

I started to feel at home with my new *Foxcatcher* family. Mark and Sunrise and I were chatting it up and laughing, and Sienna Miller's friend/publicist and I were really hitting it off. She was funny and charming, and I think she thought I was, too, because we were really yukking it up. We instantly had a lot of inside jokes, and we were really enjoying each other's company. I clocked Sienna Miller looking at us with confusion and vague curiosity many times.

Sitting next to Mark was a real treat because he is so cool and nice, but it was also an interesting viewpoint to witness his evening from. He was nominated twice, once for *Foxcatcher* and once for *The Normal Heart*. He was brilliant in both. It just so happened that both awards he was nominated for were presented back-to-back. First came Best Supporting Actor—Motion Picture, and next, Best Actor—Television Motion Picture.

When Benedict Cumberbatch and Jennifer Aniston were announcing Best Supporting Actor, I was just beaming at Mark, applauding wildly. In my mind he was my new best friend. I was very invested in his winning. Sadly, he did not win, though I think he should have. He smiled and nodded and did the thing you do when you lose an award on live television. I could recognize that look from my own face when I lost my first Tony. He seemed okay though.

Because we were now best friends, I was already thinking ahead to his next award. *Surely they will give it to him for that,* I thought. His second category was up, and this time Jennifer Lopez and Jeremy Renner read the nominees' names. As I was smiling and clapping at him, Mark said something to me. Something that I will never forget and that made me love him forever even though I haven't seen him since the 2015 Golden Globes. He smiled at me nervously, and through his somewhat tense smile he said, "It's happening too quickly."

It's happening too quickly. It was such a simple and vulnerable thing to say to a stranger. I saw in his face, in his eyes, that he was being truthful in that moment. All the buildup to the ceremony that night, all the anticipation for the nominations weeks earlier, all the hard work of actually making the film years prior. What an odd few seconds those must have been, sitting there, wondering if he would be rewarded for his efforts with a strange little trophy given by even stranger people. The presenter did not say Mark's name for the second time that night. He maintained his smile, as did Sunrise.

I don't know why I cared so much about the Ruffalos' evening. Maybe it was their kindness when I arrived at the table, maybe it was my respect for him as an actor, maybe it was the champagne Sienna Miller's publicist/friend and I were mainlining all evening, but I felt close to Mark somehow.

It was now, dear reader, that I did something that, in the moment, seemed fine, supportive even, but that, just a few minutes later, I realized was probably wildly inappropriate. Because I sensed or maybe inferred that Mark was feeling a little down about not winning either award he was nominated for, and because he was just sitting there sort of blank-faced, I decided the best thing for me to do—as a new acquaintance of Mark's, a somewhat familiar face at best—was slowly and tenderly stroke Mark Ruffalo's back in his time of trophy loss. Why did I think I had the right to do this? I'm not sure. Did he mind? I'm not sure. Did I take anything away from the moment? Who knows? What I *do* know is that he smiled at me and said, "Thanks, man." I also know I have not received a restraining order in the last seven years, so I think I might be in the clear with the Ruffalos.

Honestly, I didn't really think about my uninvited consoling rub until about thirty minutes later when I went over to the *Girls* table and Lena asked me, "Did you rub Mark's back when he lost?" The question was asked with judgment. But I didn't care. I was an unofficial member of Team *Foxcatcher*.

As out of place as I thought I was that night, I saw several displays of humanity that made me realize that even movie stars get nervous and awkward at events like the Golden Globes. Everyone is just trying to fit in at the end of the day. Even fancy people you see on TV and in the movies.

Except Sienna Miller. She seems to be in charge everywhere. But I did get a bit of revenge that night. At one point her publicist/friend and I were laughing hard about something and Sienna said, "What are you laughing about? I feel left out!" The publicist/friend smiled and I said, "Just something silly."

Too late, Sienna! Too. Late!

HAPPY BIRTHDAY

FUCKING BIRTHDAYS. AM I RIGHT?

I am about to turn forty-four. It's not that I feel old. This isn't going to be me whining about aging, I swear. Enough gay men have done that in print already. I have reading glasses now and I hate night driving and I have thrown my back out more times than I would like to admit, but all that aside, I think I still *feel* the same. Some days I still think I even look the same. There is a lot of gray in my hair, but the hairline is still solid. There are some new lines on my face but none that really bother me enough to do anything about them. And I've lived in Los Angeles, so I know there is *a lot* I could do about them.

My body pretty much moves the same as it used to, but sometimes it takes longer for me to recover. When I was filming *The Prom*, the choreographer, Casey Nicholaw, who also choreographed *The Book of Mormon*, asked me if I could still do a move I had done in that show ten years earlier. He wanted to include it in a number called "Love Thy Neighbor." It's called a "jazz split." You throw yourself from standing into a split, but your back leg is slightly bent and then you pop back up to standing with very little help from your hands and zero help from another human. My ego got the best of me and I said, "Of course I can!" I was indeed able to do it on the day we filmed that number, but afterward I had to take a fistful of ibuprofen and ice my crotch. But I did it! I still got it! Will I be doing that at fifty-five? No. I will not even attempt it, but I do have it committed to film for posterity.

I think I am basically the same person I have always been, but forty-four seems like a new chapter. I will turn forty-four on August 23, which will also be my first day of rehearsal in London for a new musical I will be doing there. I won't know anyone in that rehearsal room, and the energy will be that of a first day of rehearsal: nerves, excitement, more nerves. I doubt anyone will be aware that it is my birthday. I am fine with that—more than fine in fact. I like the day to pass quickly and with little acknowledgment. I have had several working birthdays like that in my life. I was rehearsing on my birthday for *Pokémon Live!*, *Hedwig*, *Falsettos*, *The Book of Mormon*, and *Jersey Boys*. I was filming on my birthday for *The New Normal*, *The Intern*, and *The Boys in the Band*. I tell myself that this is the real gift, the gift of employment—especially for an actor. These were perfect days. I was distracted by doing what I love to do, and that was celebration enough.

I usually don't tell anyone I'm working with that it is my birthday. I just let it go by and treat it like it is a secret, special day for me and only me. Of course, sometimes people find out and there is a break for a cake or people are made to sing "Happy Birthday" for me, which always makes me uncomfortable. (Especially when a bunch of musical theater people do it. There's always a lot of excessive harmonizing going on.) It's a lovely gesture, but I usually feel a type of embarrassment reserved for that specific moment. I know most people work on their birthdays; I'm not suggesting this is something special. I have come to treat it like just another day because that's what it is for everyone else—just another day.

Perhaps I feel this way because my birthday is on August 23, which was often the first day of school—a cruel betrayal by the Omaha school system. It was supposed to be my special day, damn it! I couldn't start school on my special day! Lots of kids have to go to school on their birthdays, but later in the year it didn't seem as traumatic. You could bring treats to class. But on the first day of school there was no time for that. Everyone was nervous and overwhelmed and there was no celebrating. There were no snacks. Everyone was fighting a stomachache. That sort of set the tone for all my birthdays after that.

Even though most of my birthdays were ruined by school starting, I've still had some really good ones. The first birthday I remember, like *really* remember, is my fifth birthday. I was about to start kindergarten and felt like I was beginning a new adventure and moving into a new phase of my little life. I woke up so early due to my excitement that my dad was still home getting ready to go to work. I rarely saw him in the mornings, so this was a special treat. My mom and dad decided to let me open one gift that morning, but I had to wait until after dinner to open the rest. I hoped that I knew what the gift would be, but I also knew that my birthday wish list included some items that might be a long shot.

Even at five, I knew I had asked for something that wasn't typical for a little boy in Omaha, Nebraska. I had been to the store with my mom weeks earlier and steered her toward the toy aisle "just to look." But I knew I had a birthday coming up, and I figured this was my chance to tell my mom what I really wanted. We went past the Matchbox cars, the G.I. Joes, and the board games, and then we finally found ourselves in the Barbie aisle. I spotted her: Malibu Barbie. She was beautiful. She came with a bathing suit and sunglasses and, of course, a tiny brush to tame her gorgeous blond hair. I needed that Barbie. Why she spoke to me, I don't know. Maybe it was too much time watching *Knots Landing* with my sisters. Maybe it was the chance to role-play with her and act out fantasy scenes of a life in Malibu, wherever that was. I just knew I wanted her. I don't remember what my mom's exact response was, but I don't remember any tension or pushback. I was nervous because it was a "girl's toy," and I didn't know any other boys who had Barbies. My brother certainly didn't. But I told her that I wanted Malibu Barbie and that was that.

So now, the morning of my fifth birthday, given the chance to open one early gift, I was desperately hoping my new SoCal friend would be behind the Smurf paper that my mother had so lovingly wrapped the package with. I sat at the kitchen table while my father, dressed in a suit and tie, watched me as I tore it open. And there she was. Malibu Barbie. I was ecstatic. My mom had listened, and she had heard me.

I played with that Barbie all day, creating elaborate scenes where Malibu Barbie danced on the beach with friends, surfed, and brushed her hair dramatically. I didn't know where Malibu was, but I knew it was clearly magical. My family gathered for dinner that night to celebrate my birthday. My grandma and my aunt Dorothy came over. I think we had Chinese food. There were more gifts, but the only one I remember is Malibu Ken, to round out the couple. I don't know if my parents chose him to complete the set, or maybe to infuse some masculine energy into the day, but I was equally thrilled with Ken. He had a purple bathing suit and sunglasses and abs! I think my parents must have thought Ken somehow balanced out the sexual en-

ergy of Barbie, but really, all it did was make me want to
look like Ken. (I still want to look like Ken.) It was a damn
good birthday. Maybe my favorite. I was young enough to
enjoy the day for what it was, to be content with a little
extra attention and gifts and a special meal on a weekday. I
wasn't self-conscious or anxious about anything. It was just
pure joy.

And then there was last year, my forty-third birthday. I
was waiting for my mother to complete a visit at her oncologist because she had just been diagnosed with cancer
and would start chemo in a few days. I had just broken up
with my boyfriend of over two years, whom I loved more
than anyone I have ever loved. The television show I had
worked on for the past three years had just been canceled.
In short, it was a shitty day by any standard, but an especially shitty birthday. My heart hurt in every possible way.
I was happy I could be there for my mom and I tried my
best to keep the mood as positive as possible for her, but I
knew she was incredibly nervous about her diagnosis and
what the treatment for it would be like. I was also scared
and sad for my mom. I wanted to protect her and tell her it
would all be fine, but on that day, there were no answers.
My attempted cheerfulness rang hollow. The fact that it
was my birthday made my mom seem sadder. She kept
apologizing to me and I kept assuring her it was fine, and I
think as a result, we both just felt crappy. I wished we could
have just skipped the day. It felt wrong. I didn't want to

celebrate myself that day; it felt selfish. I was happy for my health, but my mother was ill and in pain. I was happy for the love of my friends and family, but I didn't have a partner to lean on. Everything was off. I decided in the oncologist's waiting room that I would just make up this birthday later.

You know when you have a really unexpected killer day? Everything goes right, you meet up with friends spontaneously and have loads of laughs, your hair is exceptionally good, and you have great sex with your boyfriend in the middle of the day just because you can? When I have those days, maybe what I should start doing—what we should all do—is claiming those days as my birthdays. Right before we go to bed, we can say to the room or to the mirror, "Today was my birthday and it was fucking awesome." It would really take the pressure off the one day we are supposed to be having a great day.

When we got home from the doctor, my seven-year-old niece, named Charlotte after my mother, asked me if I wanted to play Barbies with her. *To play Barbies.* Of course, I said yes. Charlotte has many more Barbies than I ever did, though I had a nice collection. My parents didn't stop at Malibu Barbie and Ken; there were Western Barbie (and Ken) and Golden Dream Barbie (and Ken). But Charlotte's collection includes different races, different body types, every hair color imaginable, props for days, and an obscene number of costume changes. The Barbie scene work possibilities were endless. We sat on the floor of my sister's living room and we played Barbies. There were fights and action sequences and job interviews. The Mulan Barbie and the Fashionista Ken started a boba tea truck but then had it repossessed by Pilot Barbie. I turned Astronaut Barbie into a children's talent agent and forced Meditation Barbie to audition for me with songs and dances. (Those are all real Barbies, by the way. I didn't have to make up any of that.) It was fun. It was easy. It took my mind off what the day was, or should have been. For those forty-five minutes I was five again and I was very happy. I think it also made my mom happy to see me and little Charlotte having such a good time together. And honestly, that's kind of all I needed.

Fuck it. I'm deciding it now. Maybe it won't be on August 23, 2022, but my forty-fourth birthday, wherever I am, whatever is happening, is going to be great.

I THOUGHT I WAS
A MEDIUM. . . .
I'M ACTUALLY A LARGE

IT'S CURRENTLY 9:45 A.M. IN NEW YORK CITY. I HAVE been dressed to go to the gym with my little gym bag packed since 8:30 A.M. I had a whole plan for myself today. I was going to work out first thing, go grocery shopping, and then have the rest of the day to write. It was going to be a very productive day. But then I started cleaning my bedroom. I realized I hadn't changed my sheets in a while, so I figured I should do that. You know, that's a whole process. Stripping the bed, putting the sheets in the washing machine, getting out new sheets, putting those on the bed—it takes time. Then I realized I was hungry, so I made myself some eggs while the sheets were in the washing machine. But I can't run on a full stomach, so I have to wait to digest my breakfast. If I leave now the gym will still be crowded. I'll wait until 11:00 A.M. That makes more sense. Maybe I'll go grocery shopping now! That's productive!

It's 10:30 A.M. The sheets are in the washer. I guess I could go to Whole Foods now. I find that store to be very comforting. Though I think it's odd that they sell clothing. Who is wearing those dresses? No, I need to go to the gym. It's probably not crowded at all. *By the time you walk there, your food will be fully digested. Just go to the gym now.* I need gym motivation. I'll look at really fit men on Instagram and that will propel me to the gym!

It's 10:40 A.M. That wasn't helpful. I don't feel well. Why did I look at that? No one really looks like that, right? Like no one in *real* life has abs like that. Or a chest like that. Well, Henry Cavill does. It's 7:40 A.M. in L.A.; I bet Henry is at the gym right now. He seems so disciplined. He's probably home from the gym actually. Okay, just go now! Go right now and then you'll be done with the gym and you can really start your day!

It's 11:00 A.M. My bathroom was disgusting so I thought I should clean it. I should do the kitchen, too, as long as I have all the products out. Yeah. Do that. Clean the bathroom, clean the kitchen, go to the gym, and then you can start writing. Maybe make a coffee first.

It's 11:25 A.M. Zuzanna called and we had a nice catchup. She told me that there is a new episode of *The Lost Kitchen* on the Magnolia Network. If you haven't seen it, it's a reality show about a woman in Maine who has a very fancy farm-to-table restaurant that you have to be invited to go to. You send in a postcard and this woman picks at random who gets to come. You can't even pick your own date or time, she chooses for you. It's bananas. I don't know why I find that show so comforting, but I do. It makes me want to go to Maine. It makes me want that woman to pick me. Maybe I should send in a postcard. . . . I'll go to the gym now and then watch that show before I start writing. But I still have to go to the grocery store. I know, I will order groceries from Instacart and have them delivered! The sheets still have to go in the dryer, I don't want them to get mildewy. That's a real concern. Okay, I'll wait for the sheets to be done, order my groceries, and then go to the gym. That's a good plan.

It's 12:00 P.M. These sheets are taking forever to dry. I think I smell . . . like, BO smell. How is that possible? I haven't done anything today. Should I shower? That's weird, to shower before the gym; you are going to shower there anyway. No, I'll just shower quickly. That's fine. I'll shower, the groceries will come, and then I can work out and start writing. That's the plan.

It's 12:40 P.M. I'm looking at myself in the mirror and I don't like what I see. I really need to go to the gym. I should have just gone first thing today; I would be done with it now. Have I gained weight? I think I have. This is not good. I could very easily balloon up. I have to keep an eye on that. I don't have a scale in my house. I have never owned a scale. Oprah says it's not necessary. It's how you look in the mirror that matters. How your clothes fit. Oh! That's what I'll do, I'll try on my blue suit pants to see if they still fit!

It's 12:50 P.M. They kinda fit. I don't think I can sit down, but they buttoned. I really need to go to the gym. But I have to wait for the groceries. Maybe I should order some wine from Drizly to be delivered while I'm waiting. Sean might come over tomorrow, so I should have something here. Okay, I'll order some booze while I am waiting for the groceries, and then I'll go to the gym and then I'll start writing.

It's 1:00 P.M. The groceries should be here by 2:00 P.M., so I can unpack them and then work out. It's still early in the day and the gym will be empty. This is a good plan. I should call my sister Natalie. I know she's working from home today. That would be good. Call her while you are waiting, get your stuff all unpacked, and then work out. Done!

It's 2:05 P.M. Natalie just told me that one of our grade school teachers was arrested for drug possession. I'm shocked! She always seemed like such a square. I guess you never know what's going on with people privately. In this case it was meth. The groceries still aren't here. But the wine arrived. How were they so fast? I guess I'll watch *The Lost Kitchen* while I am waiting and maybe try to write while it's on in the background. It's not like that show requires too much attention. I also have to fold those clean sheets. I can't just leave them in the dryer to wrinkle. I wish

I had an ironing machine like Martha Stewart. I saw her do that on her show years ago. It seemed like a fun chore. I guess I could just iron the pillowcases? That's easy enough. And I have a couple of shirts I should do, too. Okay, I'll iron, watch the show, and then go to the gym. If I'm there by 3:00 P.M. I'll still miss the postwork crowd. That's better anyway. Okay. That's the plan.

It's 2:45 P.M. The ironing went well. I find that a very meditative chore. I think I get that from my grandma. *The Lost Kitchen* is ridiculous. Who does this woman think she is, just picking and choosing restaurant guests like she's God. And who knew there were so many types of edible flowers? I'm also confused by her business hours. She always seems to be in a field harvesting wild berries. Is that restaurant only open one day a week? It seems like it. She's always so stressed about the "serving." It's a restaurant, hon, people are just going to keep coming!

It's 3:15 P.M. I should call my mom. That would be good. I can call her when I am walking to the gym. That's good. It'll be a quick chat but at least we can catch up a little.

It's 3:30 P.M. The groceries arrived. It took longer to put everything away than I thought it would. I started cleaning out my cabinets. How long is an open bag of pasta good for? That probably gets stale, right? It seems like a waste to throw this out though. It can't be that old. I should Google it. There surely will be something online about that. Now someone is at the door.

It's 3:45 P.M. The door was a delivery from Etsy. I ordered a weird macramé wall-hanging thing for my guest bedroom. I really want to see what it looks like.... Okay, I'll hang up the wall art, I'll put away those sheets and throw out the pasta—fuck it—and then I'll go to the gym. It's not going to be that crowded. That's fine, and then I can make dinner after I work out.

It's 4:15 P.M. I really like the macramé! But there are holes in the wall from the pictures that were there before. I should fill those in. I should just do it now because if I put it off, I'll never do it, and then some guest will be in here and be like, "Wow. I thought Andrew was more on top of it than this." I'll spackle in those holes, and while it's drying I will go to the gym, and then I can hang up the macramé. The gym is going to be a little crowded now though.... If I wait until six, the gym will be pretty empty. I should do that. That makes more sense.

It's 4:40 P.M. I wish I was better at spackling. I mean, something is going to cover the wall anyway, so it really doesn't matter, right? I need to eat something. Something light so I can still work out afterward. I just bought all those groceries but I really don't want to eat any of them. That's silly. Just make a little sandwich. Then go to the gym. Or just go now! Just go now and muscle through and then you can eat later. That makes more sense. Just go right now.

It's 5:00 P.M. I made the sandwich. I just need to wait for a minute before I work out. God, it's so dark out now. I hate how dark it gets in the winter. Walking to the gym in the dark, that's depressing. I bet Henry Cavill has worked out twice today. That seems like something he would do. Okay, you can still work out today. People work out at this time all the time. It's after work, tons of people do that. I wonder if that spackle is dry. I'll look.

It's 5:30 P.M. The spackle was dry enough, so I just went for it and hung the macramé on the wall. It looks good! I should send my sister a picture. I should also dust this room. It is very dusty. I never think to dust the headboard. Why don't I do that more often? Okay, dust quickly and then get the hell out of here! You can make it to the gym by six. That is totally acceptable. And you can still write tonight. You also have to read that script that your agents sent. Damn it. When did they send that? I should look.

It's 5:50 P.M. I have too many spam emails! Why am I on the Pottery Barn Kids email list? How the hell did that happen? I have literally never shopped at Pottery Barn Kids. The script is not that long. Maybe I should just skim it and then reply. It's only 2:50 in L.A. I can catch them before the end of the day there. Or I could read it at the gym? No, I can't run and read. That doesn't work. Skim it now quickly. Then go to the gym. You can be there by 6:30. What time do they close? Probably late. It's probably really empty at like seven. Maybe that's better? Take a little more time to read and then go to the gym. That makes more sense. That's a good plan. Read. Work out. Make dinner. Done. Great.

It's 7:00 P.M. That script was better than I expected. I should respond now. Or maybe I should wait? It's not like they instantly reply to all my emails. I can give it a moment. No, I should just write them back now. Get it off my plate. It's so dark out. . . . Is it too late to go to the gym? No, just go now! If you leave right now you can get it done. It's been a productive day but you still need to work out. You are getting bigger by the second. Just do it now.

It's 7:40 P.M. I had more emails than I'd thought. Why wasn't my phone alerting me? That's so annoying. I count on that fucking thing to do one job, and it usually fails me. I mean, it's not like the phone part even works that well! I am getting hungry again. No! Go to the gym and then you can eat. That's the plan! Go now!

It's 8:00 P.M. I can't work out now. That would be silly. I could get injured. It's the end of the day. That's when most injuries happen. Maybe I could do sit-ups and push-ups here? No, that's not going to happen. Why are you so lazy? You've done nothing today. I mean, that's not entirely true. You did do stuff, you just didn't work out. That's okay, right? You were productive in other ways. In the grand scheme of things, it's not like skipping this workout is really going to change your body that drastically. Right? You'll go tomorrow morning. That's the plan! Tomorrow! Tomorrow you have a whole plan for the day and it will start with the gym! Done and done!

WHAT WORDS CAN I GIVE YOU THAT WILL COMFORT ME?

I N FEBRUARY 2021, I DECIDED THAT I WOULD JOIN the app Cameo to raise money for the Actors Fund, which provides health care, rent assistance, mental health services, and a lot more to folks in the performance community. If you are not familiar with Cameo, I will try my best to explain it. It's an app some very smart and industrious young people invented that allows admirers of public figures (actors, singers, athletes, Real Housewives) to reach out directly and request a short video from said actor/ singer/athlete/Real Housewife for a fee. It can be for your friend's birthday, your daughter's graduation, your anniversary. You are basically hiring these people to say whatever you would like them to say.

Joining this platform for charity seemed like a great idea. In normal, pre-pandemic times, I had helped the Actors Fund raise money by taking part in live events. But since concerts and other performances wouldn't be happening again anytime soon, Cameo seemed like a way for me to offer them some support in the meantime.

I was a little nervous but mostly excited to dive into this world of Cameo. I was expecting a lot of birthday wishes and Valentine's Day videos, and there were a lot of those. I was pleasantly surprised that nearly all the requests were super respectful and well-meaning. (Except for the man who asked me to promote his homemade erectile dysfunction medication. To that I said, "No, thank you, sir.")

But there was another huge chunk of requests that I was not expecting. One that really gave me pause and made me question if maybe I was in over my head a bit here. Daily, I received multiple messages from young people, often in high school, many identifying as queer, asking for messages of encouragement. "You are okay." "You are enough." "You are going to be all right." I was surprised by this. I was saddened by this. I was also encouraged by this. When I was young, I never would have had the courage to reach out to someone like that. To ask a stranger—albeit a stranger that you might feel a connection to—for guidance. A lot of factors complicated these requests. Let's start with the obvious: I was offering a rather intimate interaction in exchange for money. For $100 a pop you could reach out to me and I would talk directly to you with a tone of familiarity. These messages are meant to be personal. Names are used; details about your school or your favorite Broadway show are all encouraged. It's false intimacy, but intimacy nonetheless.

At the same time, the experience was strangely anonymous. Yes, specific people were sending these requests, but I had no idea who they really were. Sure, they might have said that they were a teenage girl in Minnesota, but they could have been a fifty-year-old man in Florida. Some requests were wildly specific in asking for certain phrases to be used. Those requests made me nervous. What if it was a dog whistle for some group or organization I didn't agree with? Some messages were from men asking me to help them get back together with their ex-girlfriends. I don't know you, bro! She might be better off without you! What if I was making something that could be used to hurt someone or offend someone? I had my guard up while making these videos.

And most important, I didn't know the details of the recipient's life or the intricacies of their troubles. It felt trite—and honestly, a little irresponsible—to simply wish someone well. To tell them, without knowing what the problem was, "You'll be fine!" What if it wasn't going to be fine? What if they needed more specific and immediate help? Was I making things worse? Was I offering false hope?

Once I pressed send, I had no idea whether I'd actually helped the person, which made the process even more confusing for me, because I didn't understand their impulse to send these requests in the first place. I have never been good at asking for help. I remember being five and wetting my bed. Rather than telling my parents, I attempted to change the sheets myself, much to my father's surprise. I don't recall there being a ton of shame involved; it was more of a matter of practicality. I made the mess, I should clean it up. What I was going to do with the dirty sheets, I had no idea, but I knew I needed to take care of it myself.

This intense, and inescapable, sense of responsibility followed me throughout my childhood and teenage years. Sometimes it was helpful and character building and made me feel stronger for a moment. More often, it made me feel alone. I once ripped the side mirror off my mom's minivan backing down our driveway. This was something I had seen all my older siblings and my mother do at one point. It was a narrow and treacherous driveway—still is. It should have felt like a rite of passage. But instead of admitting I had joined this minor-car-accident club, I drove myself to the Chrysler dealership and had it replaced with my own money. No insurance, no questions, I just did it.

Of course my parents knew what had happened. My mother had heard the sound of cracking plastic and smashing glass as I backed down the driveway, and the mirror had clearly been replaced. But there was very little discussion about it afterward. I wanted to talk about it; I wanted some kind of reaction from my parents, but there was none.

I told myself that it was probably better that way. I returned to my usual stance: I broke something, I fixed it. It was easier. It was cleaner. It made me less vulnerable.

Various therapists over the years, not to mention self-help books and talk shows, have suggested different reasons for my behavior. There's my family: I come from rather staunch Nebraskan stock who created everything they had from very little. There had been no wealth from previous generations to usher them into comfort or success. My family carved all that out themselves. There was a pride in that, a sense of agency that I was taught to respect and value. You don't expect help, you just do it, damn it! Figure it out!

Then there's the gay factor—the "Best Little Boy in the World" phenomenon that has long pushed queer kids to overcompensate for feeling weaker or more vulnerable than other kids. For feeling less than. You study harder, you behave better, you excel at extracurriculars in ways that your peers do not. And you do it all to say: I know that I'm different, and that you might not love me anymore if you knew, but won't it be so much harder to reject me if I have all these other amazing skills? Sure, I'm gay and will bring shame upon our family and will probably burn in hell, but look at my report card! Look how well-behaved I am! Look at how well I kick this soccer ball! (I don't play sports; I never have. I shouldn't have included a sports reference. How about this instead?) Look at me playing the lead in this community theater production of *You're a Good Man, Charlie Brown*! (That feels more authentic.)

I felt that I could ease the inevitable disappointment about who I was by making myself as independent and invisible and successful as possible. It would be an insurance policy for being loved. As I write this, I'm exhausted thinking about it. It would have been so much easier to be honest, to reach out for help rather than trying to plow ahead and navigate the pitfalls of adolescence alone. If only I could have requested a Cameo from Charlotte Rae from *The Facts of Life*, or Lisa Whelchel from *The Facts of Life*, or anyone from *The Facts of Life* to tell me about the facts of life!

Every day I would sit down at my desk and record these messages, often while managing my own panic and significant mood swings. The specific requests kept coming. Every day I would get at least ten from people asking me to tell them that they were okay. That everything was going to be all right. I tried to imagine what each person might be going through, what might be helpful to say or what advice I could offer. But the truth was, I was struggling, too. The past year had been a real roller coaster of emotion for the entire world, and I was on that ride with everyone else. There were good days and not-so-good days and really awful days that blurred and stretched into a year of feeling very out of control. I had weeks where I was not okay.

Even with Broadway and film projects paused for the

moment, I was lucky that I still had some writing projects that I was actively working on. These projects gave many days shape and purpose. I would wake up, shower, and get dressed—sometimes in an overly formal outfit considering I was never seeing anyone in person—and then I'd sit in front of my computer and try my best to be creative and insightful and funny and meet these deadlines that I had. I was grateful for my health and the health of my family and friends, and I was grateful for these moments of purpose. Then the deadlines would be reached, I would turn in my work and wait for notes, and I would find myself once again with nothing to do. Socializing in person wasn't an option. Zoom calls weren't as fulfilling as they once had been. Online shopping that once had brought me such joy was leaving me numb. How many vintage-inspired Nikes from J.Crew did I need? Documentaries about serial killers that used to bring me strange comfort now just seemed, appropriately, depressing and sad. Cooking elaborate recipes from *The New York Times* left me empty when I sat down to eat them alone. But my risotto was getting better! I only had so many closets and drawers to reorganize.

So cocktail hour started earlier and earlier; five P.M. became three P.M., which became one P.M. I was drinking alone and watching way too much TV and spiraling into panic and despair about what my life was looking like and when it would all go back to the way it had been. I started forgetting things, missing business phone calls because I didn't write the times down correctly. Or worse, I started taking those calls with a cocktail in my hand. At first I thought no one would suspect it. Who would be drinking at one P.M. on a Tuesday? I could handle it. *I don't sound drunk,* I told myself. *I am fine.*

But I wasn't. I was getting progressively messier and more reckless. I was still doing my work, so I was okay, right? This wasn't a problem, right? I told myself that I was doing this because I was bored, because I lacked activity. But really it was more than that. I was lonely. I felt isolated. But the activity I was choosing to distract myself from this feeling—in this case, drinking—was making my feelings stronger rather than making them fade away. What's more, who was I to be depressed? I didn't have nearly the problems other people did. What right did I have to complain or ask for help?

But I did need help. I needed to ask someone to tell *me* that it was going to be okay. That *I* was okay. I rarely reached out for that. I went back to attempting to be the Best Little Midwestern Boy in the World and plowed ahead, self-soothing in an effort to not bother anyone. Now here I was, sitting at my desk alone, being asked to encourage strangers to keep going, to have hope, to trust that things would be okay. Could I say these things and make them sound true? I'm supposed to be an actor; that's what I do, right? I make people believe that I am someone I am not. That I feel things I don't. But this was different. I wasn't playing a part; I was essentially being hired to be me, but I was still being given a scene to play as myself with a partner I could not see, did not know, and would never hear from again.

So I looked at their script, I imagined a bit about who they might actually be and what might be going on for them, and in the end, I said what they wanted me to say but also what I wanted to hear. *Everything is going to be okay. You are all right. We will get through this.* Yes, it was vague. But for me there was still a comfort in the blanket statement of support and general positivity. I didn't get specific because I couldn't. I just had to hope that knowing that someone heard them, that someone listened and responded, would be helpful on some small level.

I started to get some repeat clients during my two-week Cameo stint. Let's call one of them "Katie." Katie would write to me and request a video, for $100 each time, about every two or three days. The script that she would propose would always involve a question about a specific Broadway show I was a part of and then end with her asking me to tell her that she was going to be okay. Katie and I developed a mini relationship during this time that grew more personal with each video. It was on the fourth video that I told her, "Katie, I really appreciate you reaching out and thank you for the support of the Actors Fund, but I am concerned that you are spending too much money on these videos and I'm not sure that I am actually being helpful to you." The next day I got her response, for an additional $100, that I was indeed helping her and money wasn't a problem.

This did not ease my tension. On the one hand, I had once paid a therapist several hundred dollars a week, sometimes twice a week, to help me, so who was I to monitor someone's spending to make themself feel better? On the other hand, unlike a professional therapist, I was offering sixty-second videos, speaking in platitudes and reassuring someone about problems I really had no knowledge of. Ultimately, I decided to err on the side of bringing comfort to those who needed more.

Unexpectedly, I found that these Cameo messages were helping me, too. I needed to hear the things that I was being asked to say. During my time on Cameo I finally found the strength and forgiveness for myself to start being honest and talking to my friends and family about my feelings, about what I was experiencing and going through. It was hard to do. I felt weak and vulnerable, and maybe worst of all, I felt human. Like a person who didn't have all the answers and needed to admit that to himself and others. Much to my surprise, the people I reached out to started talking to me in a new way. They started sharing their feelings and fears and frustrations with me. It made me feel less alone and less vulnerable and more genuinely connected to myself and those people. I was right to ask for help, and just saying it all out loud made me feel better. Not entirely fixed, but better.

I once heard Christine Ebersole say in one of her cabaret acts, "What words can I give you that will comfort me at this time?" I think that's exactly what I came to feel while making those videos.

I can say with a fair amount of confidence that I am feeling much better at the moment. I went back to regular therapy, downloaded a couple of meditation apps, read a few self-help books. Returning to a regular workout routine and being honest with myself about my own feelings have put me back on a track of healthier living and being generally happier. And on days when I am not feeling so hot, I make it a point to not shy away from that feeling. I don't try to chase it away or distract myself; I acknowledge it and try my best to move through it. There is something freeing about saying, "Well today sucks!" and then continuing on with your day.

If I am being totally honest, I've struggled with sitting in those awkward feelings for many years. Since I was a teenager, really. There have been times when I managed better than others, but it's always been there, that panic, that unease. I have a friend who said to me in the middle of the pandemic, "This pandemic is making everyone who they are with an exclamation point." It's really true. I can say that I have had to confront myself in ways that have not been enjoyable, but slowly coming out the other side, I definitely feel I know myself better, more completely. Do I always like the guy? No. But I am learning to cut him some slack. To sometimes be a little gentler with him.

If I could remake those Cameo videos for Katie, I think this is what I would say:

Katie, I hear you, hon. These past months have been fucking hard. I have felt sad in ways that I have never felt before. Then I feel guilty for feeling sad, which always leads me to feeling depressed. And that leads to acting out in all sorts of ways that usually are not healthy or helpful. But you know what? Most people are feeling the same way right now, and while that's not necessarily comforting, what it does mean is that if we are brave enough to say how we are feeling out loud, hopefully those people will also feel brave enough to share their feelings with us. I'm not a mental health professional, Katie. I tell stories and sometimes sing for a living. And while a high, belty tenor is sometimes fun to listen to, it probably won't pull you out of this funk entirely. But I do hear you, and I feel you, and I am sharing my own struggles with you. Not to burden you or try to one-up you in the depression game, but just to say, I think I get it. At least a part of it. We can be lonely and sad together, which, when you think about it, makes things less lonely and probably will make us less sad. At least it's worth a shot, right? Everything is going to be okay. We are all right. We will get through this.

Thank you for reaching out, Katie. And thank you for letting me reach out to you.

SAIGON IN THE
FINGER LAKES

WHEN IS A JOB JUST A JOB AND WHEN IS A JOB A life-changing event? I usually think every job is a life-changing event, even now. I get ahead of myself and start practicing award speeches and dreaming about real estate purchases with every offer I get. But sometimes, my friends, a job is indeed just a job. A means to pay your bills. If you are lucky, it's a chance to meet some nice folks and have some laughs in the process. This is something I learned while working in a place where I'm not sure a lot of show business lessons are usually learned: the Finger Lakes.

In 2007 I was cast in the most traditional leading man role ever in my slowly burgeoning career: Chris in *Miss Saigon*. If you are not familiar with the show, it is *Madame Butterfly* with a pop musical-theater twist. If you are not familiar with *Madame Butterfly*, here's the story of *Miss*

Saigon by way of *Madame Butterfly* by way of Andrew Rannells if I had to explain it to you while we were in an elevator: A soldier, Chris, is stationed in a postwar but still American-occupied Saigon. Chris falls in love with a beautiful local gal, Kim, who is considering trying sex work on the night she meets Chris. (Kim is really going through a hard time.) They meet, they dance, they sing, they have sex and pledge their love and devotion to each other. But then, sadly, they are separated when American forces pull out of Saigon. Years go by and Chris, assuming Kim is dead, marries someone else (typical man). But it turns out Kim is alive! And, twist! She's had his baby (Tam) and has been frantically trying to reunite with her true love. When they finally reconnect, Kim is devastated to learn that Chris has married someone else and decides the best thing to do is kill herself and leave Tam with Chris and his new wife. The end. Uplifting, right? And yet, audiences across the world love the story and the music, and *Miss Saigon* has been a massive success for decades.

I was so excited to play the role of Chris, the soldier with a short romantic attention span. It was a part I had wanted to play since I'd listened to the cast recording in high school. It was epic, it was dramatic, and it included among the first songs in the show "Why, God, Why?," which got you all weepy and then let you belt to Jesus. What young tenor wouldn't want to play that part?! Plus, I needed to build my résumé. While I had been on Broadway once, my credits were pretty thin, and I believed that playing Chris would establish me professionally as a theatrical leading man. Sure, this production would be at a theater called the Merry-Go-Round in the Finger Lakes region of New York—so far off Broadway that it involved an Amtrak train and a forty-five-minute car ride to get to it—but I was going to make the best of it. And I did. Kind of.

As I thought about how I could tell this story, I realized I could weave it together with the perspective of where I am today. But have you ever gone back and looked at letters and emails you wrote five or ten years ago to remember what you were thinking and feeling in the moment, in all its intensity and naïveté, only to realize that you didn't really know as much as you thought you did when you originally wrote it? Recently, I found my journal and the emails I sent to Zuzanna back in New York while I was on that job, and I thought it might be better to share that exact correspondence with you. Looking at it today, I am pleasantly surprised by how positive I was trying to stay, and yet disappointed by how jaded I was allowing myself to become. But I'm not going to overexplain these emails; I will just let them speak for themselves.

Dear Zuzanna,

Well, I have arrived in Auburn, New York, and let me just say, it is a fucking hole. Like, "factory shut down and now the town is a wasteland" kind of hole. What have I done? But it's only five weeks, so I am going to will myself into being okay with living in a community college dorm next to a state prison. There is a nice grocery store though, and a Domino's across the street. Tomorrow I start rehearsal and will meet the rest of the cast. So far they're all sixteen. I already feel old. Jesus! I will continue to give you updates periodically, especially when we get into rehearsals. I just keep telling myself, *This will be great. This WILL be great. THIS WILL BE GREAT!!!!!*

Love,
Andrew

Dear Zuzanna,

I started rehearsals today and I have to say, I am really excited. This group is very talented and we are moving quickly. And, I don't know, maybe it was just all the high, exciting belting the gals were doing, or maybe it was the way the sun shone on the Hearing Aid Center across the street from my bedroom, but I feel optimistic. I'm telling myself, *Hey, this isn't going to be so bad. So what if we are rehearsing next to a daycare and an Al-Anon meeting, I'm an actor, damn it!* Everything could fall apart tomorrow, but tonight, FUCK IT! I also joined the local YMCA today. It's a lovely facility and as I walked through it, I realized, "In Auburn, I'm a model!" So maybe I'll get some print work for the local deli or Planned Parenthood while I am here.

I miss you already.

Love,
Andrew

Dear Zuzanna,

Since I have been up here, I have been playing with the idea that I can be whoever I want to be with these people. No one knows me here, so I could tell them I was a devout Mormon* or a recovering speed addict or a father of two and no one would know any better. While I haven't gone that far, I have decided to be a little more aloof than usual and just observe the group for a while. It has been fascinating to say the least.

Last night was the first night the entire cast went out for drinks together. I was really looking forward to getting to know the folks I work closest with, as well as chatting with the others I never see onstage. It started off okay, general getting-to-know-you bullshit. It was funny to realize that the only thing that these

---

* Quick note from today me: an interesting choice of religion, no?

people knew about me was that I was in *Hairspray*, which went over real big in the Finger Lakes. But then people started asking me other questions, like, "I heard you are bisexual. Is that true?" and "Weren't you on some TV show?" I think it was after her third Riesling that Emily, the sweet gal playing Kim, asked me, "How'd you learn to not act so faggy?" Oh Emily! What a lamb!

I cut myself off after three Sam Adams and watched the kids spiral out of control, saying things to each other like "Oh my God! Can I feel your abs!" and "When I met you, I thought you were a total cunt." Really unbelievable stuff. My only other fun interaction was when a very drunken Emily reappeared to ask me if it would be okay if we "really made out" during our scenes together and then told me she'd had a crush on me since our callback. And she offered to have my children. Oh, and SHE'S MARRIED. Wow. I finally decided to go to bed when one of our G.I.s named Woody, yes, *Woody*, stripped down to his underwear and started playing his guitar. Have a great night, kids! Enjoy living with yourselves in the morning!

Your Mature Friend,
Andrew

Dear Zuzanna,

Rehearsals are actually going well. We had a sing-
through of the entire show yesterday and everybody is
pretty amazing. So that's nice. Emily has really pulled
it back with me. I mean, she still regularly tells me how
beautiful I am and that she loves me, but other than
that, I think we are back on a professional track. She is
awfully talented though. Someone that small, who
sings like that and cries on command, I mean, I haven't
seen that since . . . well, the last time I saw a production of *Miss Saigon*. But still! She is special.

The most exciting news of late was the day of
"press" photos we had to take at a local PORTRAIT
studio. Yes, every bride in the Finger Lakes apparently
comes to this particular studio. Oh yeah, you can also
bring your DOG in for a sitting. Fantastic. The photos
were disastrous, but luckily no one will probably ever
see them since I don't think this theater has much
reach beyond the local church bulletins.

Tonight, I am hosting an *American Idol* party for
the kids in the cast. I miss you as usual. I hope you are
doing great and that you have found the strength to
continue without me.

> Your Gone but Hopefully
> Not Forgotten Pal,
> Andrew

Dear Zuzanna,

We got into the final push of rehearsals and then all
hell broke loose. Long and short of it is, we have still
never run the entire show and we have an audience in
two hours. What the fuck, right? It will be fine, I'm
sure.

The #1 highlight of this process has been the Tam
debacle. We have gone through four children playing
Tam. Apparently, some parents have objections to their
child being screamed at onstage while one actor wields
a knife over their head and another fires blanks at
them from a starter pistol. Thank God we found two
sets of parents that care nothing for their children's
safety or mental scarring. Sadly, my favorite Tam is no
longer with us. He threatened to pee on our Kim his
last day of rehearsal, so he got fired. But he was the
cutest and more importantly, he LOVED me.

After the show tonight there will be an "Opening
Night Party" at Curley's bar and grill, where the cast
and crew get free hot wings. Do you smell that? Yes . . .
it is glamour. I hope to have many wonderful photos to
share after this event. As for the show, I will let you
know what happens. Oh, by the way, our opening-
night Tam is a four-year-old girl, whose name I have
never been clear on. She is Italian, not Vietnamese or
of any Asian heritage. So that's real problematic. But

she barely flinches when that gun is fired next to her, so she got the job!

Love,
Andrew

Dear Zuzanna,

The show opened. No one was injured and the audience seemed to enjoy it, so that's good. I didn't feel like an asshole, so that's good, too. Nothing truly spectacular happened at the party, sadly.

Our second show was a bit of a nightmare. The orchestra, I'm assuming—judging by the music they were making—decided to put on mittens and attempt to play their instruments today. I have never heard such sounds before! The "conductor" said it was because they couldn't see her. I can see her and it doesn't mean I can play an instrument, but whatever. We also have a charming stage manager who calls set moves whenever he feels like it. Two members of the crew walked onstage tonight in the middle of "Last Night of the World" and moved a table. In the middle of the song. In full light.

Common sense is not common in the Finger Lakes. Other than that, we are just running the show. Tomorrow is our first two-show day. We'll see what

kind of assholes see a matinee on a Friday. I hope you
are having a good week! I miss you!

> Love,
> Andrew

Dear Zuzanna,

Yesterday was a trying day in the Finger Lakes, let me
tell you. If you liked the story about two techies moving scenery in the middle of a love ballad, you'll love
this. If you don't know, at the end of *Miss Saigon,* Kim
shoots herself and dies. This effect is achieved by one
of our stagehands, Tammy, an avid hunter, firing a
starter pistol in the wings. Well guess what? At yesterday's matinee Kim apparently died of a stroke, because
she went down, but there was NO GUNSHOT.
When I expressed my concern to our production stage
manager, Patrick—who I assume has a time machine
that takes him back to 1992 every morning as he gets
dressed—his response was, "How did that affect you?
You let me worry about the tech side of the show."
What a prick.

We had a new Tam. TOTALLY FUCKING
WHITE. Blue eyes for Christ's sake. BLOND for the
love of God. But he didn't cry or piss himself so I
guess we should be happy.

Also, I share my dressing room with two actors: Doan, who plays Thuy, and Kevin, who plays the Engineer. Doan is fantastic. Super funny, very nice. I love him. Kevin is also nice ... but yesterday, with very limited prompting, Kevin started to tell Doan and me about the martial arts cult he was trapped in for EIGHTEEN YEARS in New York. "I didn't know there was such a thing as a Martial Arts Cult," you may say. Well, apparently there is, and it is possible to be trapped in one for eighteen years. But don't worry, he "escaped" last year. I guess this karate teacher convinced a bunch of assholes, including Kevin, that she knew this guy who was sort of a god and that this god taught her a special kind of karate that only she could teach them. And, oh yeah I forgot, this whole cult setup was also a pyramid scheme, so Kevin lost a lot of money, too. What do you say to that?

Life is hard. And we all make choices. And indeed it is, and we do. Some people make the choice to become stage managers even though they lack common sense, but they own a lot of black denim so they say, "What the hell?!" Some people choose to cast white German children as Asian refugees and hope that their features won't read in the audience. Others believe in martial arts gods and give away their life savings. I have made a choice to come to the Merry-Go-Round and spend five weeks of my life that I will never get back, doing a show where the helicopter gets more applause than the curtain call. But I will live with my choice because, at this point, I have no choice.

Love,
Andrew

Dear Zuzanna,

In case you are still interested in my dressing roommate who escaped from the martial arts cult, I have another story. Out of boredom yesterday I asked him if he had ever been in a street fight where he got to use his magical martial-arts powers. He said, "Yes. Only once. And I regret it." Well I *had* to pry. Apparently, a few years back a large woman bumped into him on the subway and it turned into an altercation during which he PUNCHED and KICKED the woman on the subway. WHAT?! Who in the hell is this person? I replied, "You beat up a woman on the subway because she bumped into you?" His response: "She was as big as I was." Horrifying.

Today is our first day off in two weeks. Much needed. Last night the cast all got together and had a little party that quickly spiraled into a game of Truth or Dare as an excuse to make out with each other. But guess what? Your friend Andrew has reached a new level of restraint. After a few too many margaritas, I knew when it was time to go back to my cell (I mean *room*), wash my face, and go to bed. Maturity!

I also met Emily's husband last night. He was visiting from Chicago. He was pretty nice. He said it was only okay that I make out with his wife onstage because I'm gay. Thank you?

> Love You, Miss You,
> Get Me Out of Here,
> Andrew

Dear Zuzanna,

Yesterday, thirteen of my cast members and I were driven around the Finger Lakes in a white stretch limo on a tour of the various vineyards in the area. Whoever said that upstate New York was not known for their wines . . . was correct. The majority of the wines we tried tasted like children's cough syrup. But by the fifth vineyard they started to taste better, so I came home with six bottles of something.

I'm ready to come home now.

> Your Homesick Friend,
> Andrew

Dear Zuzanna,

I have some things to tell you. First off apparently there is an outbreak of WHOOPING COUGH that has been reported in Auburn. Even people vaccinated against whooping cough have been affected, so . . . best of luck to me.

The cast of the Merry-Go-Round's next show arrived yesterday. The show is *Peter Pan*. I saw the gal playing Peter today and she is everything I wanted her to be and more.

Picture it: small, athletic, gymnast body, ridiculously dyed red hair cut like a small boy's, and a face that betrays her 45 plus years here on Earth. She is clearly an adult woman who has played Peter at every LORT D* theater east of the Mississippi. The best part was, as I was walking past the guy playing Captain Hook chatting her up, I heard him say, "You know, I *know* Sandy Duncan." Peter grabbed her chest and with EX-TREME conviction said, "Sandy Duncan! What a hero of mine!" That was all I needed to hear.

P.S. My dressing roommate who was in the martial arts/religious cult/pyramid scheme referred to the kind

---

* That's a very small theater, usually far from a major city, for you non-showbiz folks.

of martial arts he studied as "jazz martial arts." What does that even mean? I have to go to bed now.

Love,
Andrew

Dear Zuzanna,

It's almost here. In two more days I will be home and far, far away from this horrible town. I would like to thank you for your support throughout this ordeal. Your emails and phone calls really got me through.

I would be lying if I said this whole experience was a total nightmare. There was some good that came out of it. I got to play an adult for starters. I realized that I can do a show out of town and not be drunk every day. I realized that I don't have to be drunk every day. I made tens of dollars. I now know that when people say, "Upstate has got some really great vineyards," they are either lying or have no taste buds. I now know some-one who was in a cult . . . even if it was a weird martial-arts cult. Was it what I expected or wanted? No. But it wasn't all bad either. I'll see you back in New York very soon. I'm coming home!

Your Slightly
Wiser Friend,
Andrew

Was I whisked away to Broadway after this production? No. Was I immediately offered more leading-man roles? No. But I will say, with years of distance, I am happy that I had that experience. I learned a lot about patience and professionalism and the virtue of just getting through the okay jobs on your way to the great ones. I also realized sometimes you have to make art for yourself. It doesn't matter where it is or if it moves you up a rung on an industry ladder. If it means something to you and you have some personal or artistic growth because of it, that's the important part.

I do regret being so judgmental about the process, though. I hope that it didn't show to the folks I was working with. We had some good times in spite of all the chaos at the Merry-Go-Round. And I did love singing that score every night. That was a real highlight. Could I have just sung it with Zuzanna at karaoke and called it a day instead? Probably. But now I can speak intelligently about the vineyards of the Finger Lakes region. And that is a gift in itself.

WHAT COLOR IS
MY PARACHUTE?

———

I JUST LEFT MY LOCAL TRADER JOE'S, WHERE I FIND myself more often than I would like to admit. It's cozy there, and there is something reassuring, and strangely invigorating, about grocery shopping. I know where everything is, but there are often fun surprises, things I didn't know I wanted. I just picked up some new dish towels that I really didn't need, but they were cute and only $5.99. They sparked joy, what can I say?

As I was checking out, I asked my cashier my usual "How's your day going?" She really threw me for a loop by responding, "Actually, it's not so great." I wasn't expecting that. She wasn't fishing for sympathy; she was just being honest. I followed up with, "Well, what's going on?" She said, "Not much. It's just sort of a blah day." I was really touched by her honesty.

If I was being honest with myself, it *was* sort of a blah day. I unexpectedly had the day off from work and I didn't have much on my plate except going to the gym and grocery shopping. I was amusing myself by buying dish towels I didn't need and convincing myself that I was in a good mood because of it. Was I really in a good mood? No. I was bored, I was a bit lonely, and I was not letting myself truly experience that. If someone had asked me how I was doing, I would have said, "Great!" but that wasn't exactly true. And here was this cashier who was being brutally honest with me about her own feelings as she swiped my yogurt. I decided that I should be honest with her, and myself, as well. "I know what you mean," I said. "I'm feeling the same." We just smiled at each other and that was it. There was nothing to be done or fixed, there wasn't really a crisis or anything wrong, it was just an acknowledgment of what was happening at that moment. It was indeed a blah day.

There is a benefit to a kind of benign neglect when it comes to feelings. I can't let myself feel *everything* because I probably wouldn't get out of bed if I did. As much as I would like to just lie down on my couch, I know that it is not ultimately going to be helpful. So I make myself busy. I keep moving. I have zero interest in acquiring a sourdough starter, nor do I want to create a home gym using canned goods as weights, so I have to find my own version of productivity. Often I write, and sometimes I just iron everything in my home that can be ironed. I can turn ironing napkins and pillowcases into an event that takes hours.

I envy—and am annoyed by—people who really thrived during the pandemic. People who got fit or learned to sew or used that time we were all in lockdown to sort out their life. I was lucky that I jumped back into work pretty quickly, but I was still a real mess. While I've been more fortunate than most, and I'm grateful for that, I'm still not quite right, honestly. Sometimes, I've wondered whether it's time for a whole new life adventure. A real *Under the Tuscan Sun* shake-up! But what would my second act look like?

I was recently reminded of a night, years ago, when I was hanging out with my friend Julie Halston. We were several wines into our evening, and after listening to me vent about a recent failed audition, she asked me, "What color is your *parachute*?!" I had no idea what she was talking about. She said it again: "What color is your parachute?!" We just started laughing even though I still had no idea what she was talking about. When I got home that night, I typed the question into Google, and here's what I found on Wikipedia: "*What Color Is Your Parachute?* is a self-help book by Richard Nelson Bolles intended for job-seekers. It recommends carefully figuring out what one is best at and what one enjoys most, two things that, Bolles asserts, tend to coincide." Well hell, that seems logical! Sign me up!

I have to be totally honest. (I feel we are friends at this

point and there is no reason not to be.) I just really liked the title of the book, and from that brief description, I got the gist: Do something you love and the money and joy will follow. It's a secret weapon that you can pull out if you need it. With my minimal and slightly drunk research complete, I started to think, *What color* is *my parachute? Do I have a backup plan? Is there a skill I have that I might be able to survive on?* The short answer is no. I have no practical skills, and I have never seriously considered a backup plan.

So, on this day, as I wander home through the streets of Chelsea, Trader Joe's bags in hand, my mind also starts to wander. What would I do if I had to start all over tomorrow? What would my first move be? Where would I go? What would I do? I imagine my new life would look something like this. . . .

It begins, naturally, in New York. I am jobless and hopeless—two things I have been often—and I decide that I must move on. Real estate in New York State is too volatile, so I have to leave the tristate area. I decide to go north. I think the best option is Maine. I have only spent one four-day trip there, but I romanticize it in a special way. I like that it's cold in the summer and that there's a sternness to the locals. They are proud and miserable at the same time, and I enjoy that. I don't really know cities there, but I would pick a small town on the water. And I want it to be a "town," not a "city." A place where the mayor also owns a coffee shop and everyone is a member of the fire department. It's like the nineties TV show *Northern Exposure*, except I'm not a doctor. I am still the lead of the show and John Corbett is still a DJ, but he's desperately in love with me. I think this town is called Cheddar Bay Harbor Port. That sounds right to me.

As I have mentioned, I have no practical skills. It would take too long for me to learn to cut keys or repair a windowpane. I will have to do something radical. Something bold. Luckily, I have had this secret plan in my back pocket for years. It's something I developed decades ago when I was feeling really sad.

I like to cook, but I am not a great baker. Baking, of course, is a much more exact art, one that depends on strict measurements and patience. Cooking, on the other hand, you can kind of wing. If you fuck up, you can fix it by adding cheese or chopped chives. Now, I don't know why, but I feel like a great combo of baking and cooking is scones. A scone seems like a nonsense baked good to me. What the hell is it? A flat, hard muffin? A dehydrated cupcake that got in a fight? Plus, people just start shoving whatever the fuck they want into scones. Savory scones, sweet scones, whatever's clever you can pack into those little bastards. Therefore, I feel like scones would be the perfect thing for me to tackle. I would open a scone shop in Maine. But I would spell it *Scone Shoppe* because it's folksier.

But my scones won't be enough. I need another hook to get those mean Maine locals to come in. While the vast majority of my marketable qualities lie in musical theater—including an in-depth knowledge of the creation of the musical *Sunset Boulevard*—I also have taste. Especially the perceived impeccable taste of a childless gay man who has lived in New York. I could convince a lot of people that something is valuable or fashionable just because I am tall and wear Lacoste polos. Vintage furniture . . . that would be another thing I could sell. I could scour estate sales of dead Mainers and then create a well-curated vintage furniture store tailored to weekenders and wandering gays in Maine.

Yes, scones and vintage furniture. That is my new career. And it will be called . . . *Sconiture* (*Scone-ih-chure*). Okay, the name could use some work, but it'll do for this fantasy. You can come in for a bacon/raspberry scone, but you might leave with a 1965 ottoman! Or maybe you are in the market for a 1970s record cabinet but then you also have a hankering for a buttercream/short rib/Asiago scone! We have it all at Sconiture! I become a fixture in the town quickly. The gruff locals all take to me but they are not effusive about it, which is fine by me because I don't necessarily want to host dinner parties, but I do like getting invited to them.

One day during the Cheddar Bay Harbor Port Summer Food Festival, I am welcoming guests into the store and giving away samples of my signature strawberry/feta/potato scones, when in walks the town's mayor, who also owns a coffee shop and is the town's fire chief. He looks like a 1970s Paul Newman and exudes the energy of a 1950s Paul Newman and the kindness of a 1990s Paul Newman. He's romantically shy but politically aggressive, and he's very vocal about my cooking/baking. He loves the fact that I have infused some glamour into Cheddar Bay Harbor Port. (He has a midcentury sideboard from Sconiture currently on hold.) I haven't given him a name yet. Let's say . . . Paul Newman. I know it's not imaginative, but I find it's best to be direct when fantasizing. Paul is impulsive and asks me to go to the outdoor concert/community softball game that is happening that night. Carly Simon's niece is performing and pitching. I am uncharacteristically demure and agree to go.

The concert/game is great. Carly's niece does a fine cover of "Haven't Got Time for the Pain," and she pitches that thing where a lot of batters strike out. (I don't know a ton about sports.)

The small-town excitement, the lobster rolls, the sound of a Carly Simon cover . . . Paul and I can't help it, we fall in love. "Andrew," he says through tears—but not too many, just like a misting, because I really don't care for crying in any setting—"let's get married. Please do me the honor of being my husband. I will make you happy and I will always love you, and if one day in the next couple months you are tired of making scones and selling furniture, I am also really fucking wealthy. You and I can just hang out and we can have a bunch of sex, but sex that is great and doesn't take a super-long time, and then you can tell me why *Into the Woods* is the most perfect musical all day if that's what would make you happy. Because I know it would make me happy. Did I mention that I love you?"

I brush my bangs out of my face and I stand with arms akimbo, hands on my waist, which is smaller than usual, and I say, "Paul Newman . . . of course I will marry you. I've loved you since the moment I saw that you look like the real Paul Newman and I knew you held a public office. The wealth is just a bonus. I love you, I love you, I love you."

Then we get married, and I guess I just coast the rest of my life in a house on the water with a guy who loves to kiss me and hold my hand; who doesn't get too hot when he sleeps, because I do; and who likes murder-y TV documentaries and British shows that center on a complicated female lead who is probably a detective—basically anything *Broadchurch* or *Happy Valley* adjacent. We like to cook. We like to have dinner parties when we feel like it, and we have the best house at Halloween. We don't actually speak to the children who come to the house, but we have amazing treats and we have a bar with bespoke cocktails for parents. Everyone loves us!

Paul and I have a tradition where we spend Christmas together alone. Our ritual starts on Christmas Eve. We send our gifts to our families and then we cook an elaborate meal for each other. We get dressed up in our favorite suits and then we toast with expensive champagne to our lives together and the fact that—as we learned from a consultation with a reliable local psychic—we will die together at the exact same moment and will literally never be without each other.

I am feeling content in Cheddar Bay Harbor Port with Paul Newman in a house that looks like a midcentury gay fantasia in the woods of Maine. It turns out that it was a great decision to leave show business. I followed my gut and I knew exactly when to call it quits. I am actually happier now than I ever was in New York or Los Angeles. Yes, yes, I did throw a rather heavy Baccarat-inspired decanter at our flat-screen when I saw that the little boy from *Young Sheldon* had won a Tony Award for a pop musical based on Chernobyl. But that was passing rage. Did I kick through a screen door when it was announced that Jonathan Groff got a Kennedy Center Honor? Yes, yes, I did. But Paul Newman was supportive and is handy around the house, so all those issues were fixed quickly.

I think I could be genuinely happy in that life. . . .

Maybe one day I'll try, but for now I guess I'll stick around New York City a bit longer. Maybe hit the Trader Joe's again later.

Do you think it's weird that when I have these fantasies, I ultimately end up succeeding wildly and falling in love, but with a realistic grasp of my own insecurity and self-doubt?

You're right. I don't think that's weird either. I think it's correct. If our escape fantasies aren't a happy place of refuge, then what's the fucking point?

This might be my most achievable fantasy yet. Check in with me in ten years. If you can't find me, I'll be at Sconiture. Come find me! Your first blueberry/chorizo/cream cheese scone is on me, and I'll toss in a vintage Holiday Inn ashtray, too!

UNCLE OF
THE YEAR

―――

A S A CHILD I DID NOT ENJOY BEING A CHILD. I DID not enjoy the company of other children. I always wanted to be a grown-up and be around grown-ups. I just couldn't relate to other kids. In the third grade I was the only kid who said his favorite movie star was Betty Grable.

Now, part of this is the gay thing. As a gay kid you often live in fear of being found out, of other people knowing what you know, which is that you are different. I knew I was different at age five, when I desperately wanted to be Michelle Pfeiffer in *Grease 2*. (If you know me at all, you didn't honestly think I would write another book and not mention *Grease 2,* did you?) I suppose I was really afraid of the other kids. They call you names, they judge you, they shut you out. It doesn't take a PhD in psychology to theorize that if you are a kid who does not like other kids, you might turn into an adult who does not like being around kids. And so, as an adult, I moved to New York, I found like-minded adults who made me feel safe, and I finally put childhood and children behind me.

And then . . . my siblings started having children.

First it was my sister Julie, then my sister Becky, then Julie again, Becky again, and my brother Dan not far behind with two of his own. Soon after, my sister Natalie had two children, and finally, Julie adopted two more. I am now an uncle to ten children. Because they all live in Omaha, I don't get to see them very often. But there are visits to New York and holidays in Omaha, so I have developed a relationship with them as the faraway, but hopefully fun, Uncle Andy. (Please don't say, "guncle." I feel like that really infantilizes the gays. We don't need to be cuter than we already are.)

I was very conflicted about my siblings' having kids. On one hand, I was happy for them. The kids are cute! The kids are sweet! The kids are loud as hell, but I don't see them that often, so it's not really my problem. But on the other hand, with each baby born, I started to drift further and further away from my siblings. Our family as I knew it was changing and shifting, and I felt like I was losing my place in the brood.

Joining them in Minivanland has never really been an option. Yes, I've had a string of relationships, but they've never made it past five years. In my longest relationship, with Mike, we owned a home together, we traveled for the holidays together, we made a life together. But the idea of having children with him was never really on the table. First of all, as a gay man who grew up in the nineties, it had never seemed possible to me. When I was in my twenties, I knew a handful of gay couples who had kids, but they were pretty rare and had a sense of duty about parenting. One couple inherited children from a drug-addicted sister who couldn't care for them. Another fostered children whom literally no one else would care for. There weren't gays like there are today, who have kids because they "think it will be fun" or because they "want to have a legacy," or as one gay dad I met put it, "How many more boozy brunches can we have?"

As Mike and I were breaking up, more and more friends started to have children through surrogacy. But our relationship was always a bit rocky. We knew we couldn't bring a child into the world without the proper stability. Plus I was working on BroadWAY! Where would my baby be while I was doing eight shows a week? In the stage manager's office making an understudy rehearsal schedule? In the wig room learning how to hot-roll a lace-front? It was just never something I thought about.

So I focused on what seemed like the next best thing: being a good uncle to my ten nieces and nephews. I had this idea that I would be like a male Auntie Mame (Uncle

Mame, I guess?). A fabulous presence in their lives who would introduce them to culture and new experiences and, as they got older, be the sounding board that their parents could not be. I imagined bailing them out of jail, driving them to abortions, paying for rehab. Why were my nieces and nephews so troubled in my imagination? Good question! I guess because I wanted to swoop in and save them in times of crisis but not actually be responsible for them on a day-to-day basis.

While none of my nieces and nephews has ever gone to jail, or to rehab, they have made lots of trips to New York to see me in shows and concerts. Each time they've visited, it's been exciting to have them here and to know that they were seeing Uncle Andy onstage doing what he loves and making a living from it. Maybe it inspired them, I don't know. It was also probably confusing that Uncle Andy, who came home for Christmas every year, was doing a split in a Farrah Fawcett wig as Hedwig in front of a thousand people on Broadway. I think my persona has always been a little muddied in that way. I have a whole other life that exists without them, and I'm probably very different in New York than I am at home.

To be honest, when they visited, I wasn't great with them. I didn't know what to do with kids in Manhattan. I mean, there are the obvious things, like seeing the Statue of Liberty and the Empire State Building and M&M's World in Times Square—but that shit is exhausting. Especially when you are doing eight shows a week and then waking up early in the morning to play tour guide.

Because of this additional job on top of my real job, I was often short-tempered or impatient with my family. I remember one trip that my brother Dan's family took to New York. My nephew Nathan, who was probably about six at the time, decided to lie down in a crosswalk outside the 9/11 museum and wouldn't get up. My brother and sister-in-law were about a block ahead of us, so I was left to deal with him. After a few increasingly desperate attempts to convince him to walk, I finally settled on saying, "Nathan, don't be an asshole. Just get up." To my surprise, he did. We walked in silence until we caught up with my brother, at which point Nathan said, "Uncle Andy just called me an asshole." It was not my finest moment.

There were things I was good at, though. I excelled at fun with them. I could be silly, and I made them laugh. I would speak in weird accents when talking to a waiter or break into an impromptu dance while waiting for an elevator. But at the end of the day, it was their parents that they wanted. And I was all too happy to give them back. I was just their fun uncle who played pretend for a living and who was exhausted from pretending to be Uncle of the Year in his downtime as well.

As I started working on higher-profile jobs on Broadway and TV, I could tell my nieces and nephews got a kick out of seeing me on billboards and talk shows. I brought my nephew Gavin with me to *The Tonight Show* and he got to play with a baby tiger backstage. I mean, that's some cool uncle shit right there! But for the most part my work never seemed as important to them as it did to me. I couldn't exactly show them an episode of *Girls* or *Black Monday*. A couple of them saw *The Book of Mormon,* but that led to tricky conversations and questions like "What's a fuck frog?" Uncle Andy rarely did kid-friendly fare.

Eventually, I started doing more kids' animation in the hopes that it would gain me points with them. I played a unicorn on *Sofia the First,* and I jumped at the chance to play a singing mummy on *Vampirina.* I thought, *Well, at least this is something I can show them.* I think it mostly confused them, though. Explaining show business to kids is tricky. "Why is Uncle Andy's voice in a stuffed toy?" "Why does that lady we don't know want to take a picture with you?" I didn't know how to explain a lot of it, and neither did their parents.

As the kids grew, I was able to develop my own relationship with each of them. We could talk about different things and trade notes about TV shows we were watching or books that they were reading. Our visits were mostly brief, so I can't say I was ever really able to form a truly close bond with any of them. The distance made it hard to find that consistency. I wanted to be closer with all of them, but despite my best efforts, I found myself unable to figure out how to crack the kid code. I never worried too much about it, though. I always had a new audition, another night out with friends, or a trip with Mike to keep me busy.

When Mike and I broke up and I was once again visiting Omaha alone, I felt like an outsider. While we had been off traveling and buying midcentury furniture together, all my siblings had built families of their own, filled with traditions and jokes that I wasn't part of. I felt like an interloper. I didn't fit into any family anymore.

These days, I see my siblings less as my siblings and more as parents, moms and dads who are running households and keeping little humans alive. They are completely different people with their families in many ways, and they need to be. I understand that. And watching them parent is fascinating. Their styles are all wildly different from one another's, and different from how our parents raised us. It's weird, but sometimes when we all talk about our childhoods it's as if we had five different parents even though we were all raised in the same home. Memories of how my dad was or what my mom said, even within the same situation, vary.

In recalling events from our childhood with my siblings, I've realized that as a parent you can't control how kids will remember things. Will my nephew Nathan think of my calling him an asshole as funny or scarring? (Don't worry, he thinks it's funny. I just asked him.) But that could have gone either way, and it was a moment of impatience that I put no thought into. Of course I wouldn't usually call a child an asshole to his face, but it just flew out of my mouth.

Again, I am my mother Charlotte's son. My mom once told me as a child that if I touched the reset button on the outlet in the bathroom it would burn down the house. She has no recollection of this, but I still remember it today. When I asked her about it, she said she was probably just distracted and ultimately didn't want me near the outlet, so in that moment, that was the best explanation. I get that now, but for years I was afraid of the reset button. I always wondered, *In what world would you need a button to specifically burn down your house?* I had follow-up questions for my mom, but I never asked them.

I've thought about that moment a lot over the years and have often felt anxious about what I might say, or do, as a parent—and how that would affect my kids. And for most of my adult life, I successfully avoided confronting these fears—until I started dating Tuc.

Handsome, dashing, funny, sexy Tuc.

Who has two children.

How do I do this? What if they hate me? What if I don't know what to do?

Tuc assured me that we could take this slowly. I didn't have to come flying in and have all the answers; we could figure it out together. I had never spent so much time with kids before, certainly not when you couldn't just pass them off to their parents if things got challenging. In this case, the kids were always around. There was no parent to send them home to because the parent was the person next to me in bed at night.

After dating someone with children, I began to see why people want to have them. There are moments of joy and moments of love, and I have been told by many a parent that those moments, even if they are few and far between at times, make the whole process worth it. That all the screaming and wrestling a child into a car seat and all the messes, the diaper changes, the vomiting, the constantly telling you how bored they are or daily meltdowns when they don't want to eat the food you just lovingly prepared— *all* that goes away when your child smiles at you or says, "I love you."

Intellectually I understand this. Practically speaking . . . I do not, because I do not have my own children. My boyfriend's children and I never really got to that place of simple joys. Which I totally understand. I was not their parent, I was their dad's boyfriend, and I know enough to know that does not immediately endear you to the children. I have enough friends whose parents divorced and dated other people to know how tricky that position is.

I don't love feeling like a failure. Who does? I tend to stay away from experiences at which I don't think I will naturally excel. That's not to say I don't try new things, but if I end up crying or injured or both after trying, that tends to be the last time I try that experience. But I did want to try this time. I wanted to try hard. I did want to be good at this role I had been presented with as a possible second father figure. I didn't want to run from what could be an opportunity. What if my presence could benefit the kids? What if I had something worth sharing? What if this was the thing that I was missing in my life? What if, as it was for millions of other people, parenthood was the thing that would go on to define me and give my life purpose and make me a less self-centered person? I had to put aside my discomfort with not nailing this on the first try and keep trying. I also had to figure out why this particular experience scared me so much.

I think part of the reason that the idea of parenthood really freaks me out is that I have a mother who was very good at it. Like exceptionally good at it. She had five kids to juggle, and I am certain there were plenty of times that seemed like five too many. I honestly don't recall any moments when I felt like I needed more of her time. She was always there for me and always managed to make me feel like I was special to her in a way that the others weren't. I imagine all my siblings felt that way, and the fact that she was able to make us all feel seen and focused on is quite a feat. She was a very active mom at our grade school, always there to volunteer on field trips or at classroom parties, always baking cookies to take to school or coming in the middle of the day to an all-school mass that I was an altar boy at. My mom was there to support us in any way that she could.

I counted on her presence, I depended on it, and more often than I would like to admit, I took it for granted. She made it seem easy. She made it look like she enjoyed it all. As an adult I know that simply could not be the case. I know that there had to be days when she just wanted to say fuck it and stay in bed or sit on the couch watching *Guiding Light*. I know there were days when a boozy lunch with friends would have been more enjoyable than serving hot dogs to a bunch of kids on a third-grade class trip to the zoo. But she did it. She always showed up.

My mom, Charlotte, was launched into motherhood in 1969. That's what a lot of ladies did, especially in the Midwest, at that time. Her professional options in the 1960s were largely teacher, motherhood, and convent in Omaha. She made it clear that being a mom was her job, it was a vocation, something she always wanted to do. She excelled at it. Luckily for me, after three pregnancies and one miscarriage, she had me because she wanted to expand her family even more.

There are so many difficult jobs in the world: firefighter, doctor, soldier, sanitation worker, teacher, the people who work at the Brentwood Country Mart and have to deal with those patrons. The list goes on and on. Then there are jobs that are also difficult but are tackled by choice: swimsuit model, person who makes crafts on Etsy, and, possibly most common, parent.

Over the years, I've had a lot of time to process my options and I've come to the conclusion that, unlike my mom, I don't want to start a family. Personally, I think the straights could take a page from the gays here and take the time to figure out if parenthood is something they really want to do. It's a lifetime commitment! I'm in my forties and I'm still bothering my mother with nonsense every day! (Sorry, Charlotte.) Just like I wanted to be an actor, she wanted to be a mother, and we both put all our heart into it. We each had our vocation. Being raised by my mom (and my dad) showed me what devoted parenting really looks like. You have to be all in all the time. That's what scares me so much. What if I can't be all in? What if I don't want to?

"What are your markers of time?" Tuc once said to me. We were in the middle of a tense game of Are We Breaking Up? Years before we met, at the age of forty-five, he'd found himself with a successful acting career, newly single, and desperately wanting to start a family. It was something he had always wanted and so, with the help of modern science, he had twins on his own. This made him incredibly happy. He had the family he had always dreamed of. He couldn't imagine his life any other way.

"What do you mean?" I replied.

"If you don't have children, how do you mark the passage of time in your life? You have no solid anchor to mark time."

I thought about what he said, but I disagreed. I had many markers of time. Maybe they didn't look like his, but I had them. Opening nights, trips all over the world, falling in love, falling out of love, time with my friends and family. I had my own markers of time, and I was really happy with them.

I realized as he said that to me how different we were. How differently we each pictured what a well-rounded life looks like. There wasn't a right or wrong picture—everyone gets to decide that for themselves. In this case, our pictures just didn't match up. This wasn't being mad at your partner because you still, after being asked six times, don't want to play golf with him, or because he doesn't want to watch a marathon of *Curb Appeal: The Block* with you. This was much bigger than that. The future and present of two other lives had to be considered. That was something I definitely couldn't fail at.

My relationship with Tuc and his kids is evolving and changing constantly. There is a fear in not knowing the ending but also a beauty in trusting we are finding our way.

I'd like to think that I mostly do well with the kids. I am far from perfect and often at a loss. The experience of trying to be a stepparent reminds me of what I'd always known: I don't excel with kids. And I like to excel at everything I try to do. I really spiral about this. What does it say about me that I can't connect with children? Does that mean I'm a bad person? A selfish person? Am I lacking some gene that prevents me from having that kind of love?

My therapist says no. He tells me that not everyone is cut out to do that job, nor should they be. I still have pangs of regret that I am not more adept at parenting, at uncle-ing.

What I am trying to tell myself now is that I can only be who I am, right? I know my limits. I'm not going to be Auntie Mame or Julia Roberts in *Stepmom*, and I don't need to be. More honestly, I don't want to be.

I realize now that all the social progress that the LGBTQIA community has made has also brought new pressures. For perhaps the first time, marriage and children are beginning to shape what people believe a successful relationship looks like, what it means to be an adult. I was lamenting this to Zuzanna recently, after a reporter asked me if I would get married one day and start a family "now that it's legal." I told her about the unexpected anxiety this created in me, and she looked at me very flatly and said, "No shit. That's what it's been like to be a woman for forever." Touché. The more I talk to people about this— friends, sometimes strangers—I realize that there are more of us out there than I thought.

And as far as my nieces and nephews are concerned, I love them very much. I am the uncle who plays pretend for a living, who writes stories for a living, and who lives in New York and will take them to see *Wicked* and to have dinner at Joe Allen and sometimes curse in front of them inappropriately. If they're LGBTQIA, I hope they grow up always believing that having children is possible, and maybe one day, unlike me, they'll want kids of their own. But, either way, when they're older, I'll encourage them to think more broadly about what their world can look like, what their lives can be. To not just do something because everyone tells them they should, or tells them they have to in order to be an adult.

That's my role. That's my job.

I'm not Auntie Mame. I'm Uncle Andy.

ACKNOWLEDGMENTS

———

Writing this book took a lot of support and patience and I'm not certain that I was always worthy of it.

Christie Smith, Bill Clegg, and Matt Inman, thank you for reading countless drafts and sharing your insight and wisdom with me.

Zuzanna Szadkowski, thank you for being you.

Sean Dooley, Rachel Glickman, and Jill Madeo, thank you for your love and understanding as I tell these stories that often involve you.

Tuc Watkins, your generosity and love have truly changed me as a human and I will be forever grateful to you for it.

My family, especially my mother, Charlotte, have put up with a lot from me over the years and continue to do so. I am extremely lucky to be a Rannells and you all remind me of that every day.

Most important: Tess, Claire, Rachael, Nathan, Kyra, Megan, Gavin, Edward, Charlotte, and Olivia, I know that I am often a flaky uncle who misses holidays and important events, but please know that I love you all very much. It is a privilege to watch you grow into the intelligent and undeniably cool humans you are.

———

ANDREW RANNELLS is an actor, a singer, a performer, and the author of *Too Much Is Not Enough*. A Tony, Drama Desk, and Critics Choice Award nominee and Grammy winner, he originated the role of Elder Price in *The Book of Mormon* and has starred in *Hedwig and the Angry Inch*, *Hamilton*, *Falsettos*, and *The Boys in the Band*. On the small screen, he has appeared in *Girls*, *The New Normal*, *Big Mouth*, *Black Monday*, *Welcome to Chippendales*, and *Girls5Eva*. Rannells's film credits include *A Simple Favor*, *The Intern*, *The Boys in the Band*, and *The Prom*. He has published essays in *The New York Times*, and he made his directorial debut adapting one of his own essays for the anthology series *Modern Love*.

Instagram: @andrewrannells

ABOUT THE TYPE

———

This book was set in Caslon, a typeface first designed in 1722 by William Caslon (1692–1766). Its widespread use by most English printers in the early eighteenth century soon supplanted the Dutch typefaces that had formerly prevailed. The roman is considered a "workhorse" typeface due to its pleasant, open appearance, while the italic is exceedingly decorative.

"Candid, funny, crisp . . . honest and tender about lessons of the heart." —*VOGUE*

ANDREW RANNELLS

TOO MUCH IS NOT ENOUGH

A MEMOIR OF FUMBLING TOWARD ADULTHOOD

With a new afterword

"[Rannells] verbalizes feelings of insecurity with shocking poise. . . . This is certain to resonate with all those brave enough to leave their comfort zones in pursuit of their dreams."

—Booklist

 CROWN
NEW YORK

Available wherever books are sold

DOB, J L
3750
May 17, 2024
3328193011505057   Uncle of the year : & oth

DOB: L

3/20/7̶5̶

May 17, 2024

335483304420521 Uncle of the year. 8 oht